3°°

CHINESE STYLE

CHINESE STYLE

Interiors · Furnitures · Details

Text by Zhu Wen
Photographs by Liu Shenghui

Better Link Press

This book is edited and designed by the Editorial Committee of *Cultural China* series

Managing Directors: Wang Youbu, Xu Naiqing
Editorial Director: Wu Ying
Editors: Yang Xiaohe, Susan Luu Xiang

Text by Zhu Wen
Photographs by Liu Shenghui
Translation by Yawtsong Lee, Jingwen Zhu

Cover and Interior Design: Yuan Yuan

ISBN: 978-1-60220-007-4

Address any comments about *Chinese Style: Interiors · Furnitures · Details* to:

Better Link Press
99 Park Ave
New York, NY 10016
USA

or

Shanghai Press and Publishing Development Company
F 7 Donghu Road, Shanghai, China (200031)
Email: comments_betterlinkpress@hotmail.com

Printed in China by Shenzhen Donnelley Printing Co., Ltd.

1 3 5 7 9 10 8 6 4 2

Contents

Preface

Chinese style interior design employs distinct decorative techniques, materials and elements to create interiors that reflect the essence of Chinese culture and its aesthetic preferences.

Chinese interior decoration evolved from a classically traditional style that is unique in its graceful designs in space planning, materials, colors and furnishings. It occupies a glorious chapter in design history, with a dazzling array of achievements grounded in a rich Chinese culture. However, centuries of prolonged self-imposed isolation from the outside world, perennial war and strife, extreme economic and technological backwardness stalled progress in Chinese interior design. In sharp contrast, during the same period, Western countries rapidly developed in all fields, not the least in interior design wherein Western style became the dominant aesthetic worldwide. As late as ten to twenty years ago interior design in China was still rife with blind copying and imitation of overseas design styles, to the extent that the heritage of traditional Chinese design was almost completely eclipsed. Fortunately, in recent years, this state of affairs has come to the attention of many talented people, both in and outside the field of interior design in China. These individuals are utilizing advanced technology and increasingly experimenting with contemporary Chinese style interior designs that give equal attention to the aesthetic tastes of modern society and traditional culture. Combined that with the best of Western design, Chinese style design is making a quiet breakthrough. These explorations do not stoop to the superficial expression of Chineseness achieved by a mechanical aggregation of traditional design elements. Rather, they seek the expression of the intrinsic values of traditional culture based on a firm grasp of the Chinese design techniques and aesthetic principles in space planning and the use of materials, colors and furnishings.

This book has been conceived in this spirit. Its purpose is two-fold. First, it tries to sort out the genesis of traditional Chinese interior design, giving the reader a complete picture of its formation and its characteristics, by tracing its cultural roots—its relationship to ancient Chinese philosophy, traditional art forms and local customs. The book then goes on to describe some mix-and-match approaches that have become features and trendsetters in Chinese interior design in recent years. This will give the reader a clearer picture of the major design techniques and of the current outlook of interior design in the country. To offer practical advice and guidance for DIY designers, Chapter 5 discusses, with the help of plenty of pictures, the most effective and easiest ways to give one's living space an instant Chinese look and feel after applying a few simple design touches with furnishings, materials, decorative accessories and interior colors.

Traditional Chinese interior design played an important role in traditional Chinese art and culture. It will no doubt have a bright future thanks to the efforts of designers, experts and scholars of the country. As someone committed to this endeavor, I have written this book, knowing my limitations and the book's inevitable imperfections, in the hope that it will generate genuine interest and stimulate meaningful discussion and reflections, and last but not least, that it will prove helpful to readers fascinated by Chinese culture and Chinese-style interior design.

On facing page Although the stark modern furniture here stands in sharp contrast to the elegant traditional architecture, they have the same sober color tones, which produce a harmonious decorative effect.

Chapter 1
Traditional Philosophy
in Chinese Interior Design

Like any other cultural vehicle, interior design, as an expression of the resident's interests, tastes and aspirations, can indirectly reflect the culture and thinking of the era and society. Traditional Chinese-style interior design has unquestionably played an important role, consciously or otherwise, in showcasing the spirit of traditional culture through its lively artistic expressions.

Confucianism, Buddhism and Taoism, the philosophies and religions founded two millennia ago by Confucius, Sakyamuni, and Laozi (also known as Lao Tzu), respectively, are jewels in the crown of classical philosophy and wisdom. They are also the three major building blocks of traditional Chinese culture. A "syncretism of three philosophies and religions" with Confucianism in the dominant position, complemented by Buddhism and Taoism, gradually took shape in China's traditional thinking and culture through its long history. A popular quip quite aptly reveals the profound impact the Confucian, Buddhist and Taoist teachings have had on ordinary Chinese people: "When your career thrives and you can make a difference in society, you follow Confucian teachings; when your career loses steam, you retire to the mountains and practice Taoism; when you lose all hope and would like to take a monastic vow, you can always fall back on Buddhism." Clearly the three schools of thought have interpenetrated each other to become part of the underpinnings of the Chinese national identity.

Just as a country's history is said by some to be found on the dinner table of ordinary folks, interior design, as an art form intimately bound up with the daily life of ordinary people obviously offers a glimpse into the culture of the times.

Evidence of the influence of the three philosophical systems on traditional Chinese-style interior design can be seen in "Confucian-elegant" interior spaces, which employs decorative techniques and forms favoring square shapes and a symmetrical look, to interpret the essential Confucian concepts of "humanity, righteousness, rituals, knowledge and trustworthiness." Taoist ideals of "communion of man with nature" and "inner serenity and do-nothingness" are achieved in "simple-elegant" living spaces. "Un-worldly" decorative styles are used to pursue the transcendent Buddhist ideals, such as "seeing through the earthly world and waking up to the truth of life and death." And just as Chinese thinking draws its inspiration from an organic combination of the three philosophical systems, traditional Chinese interiors often exhibit a confluence of all three influences.

Another major influence on traditional Chinese architecture is *kan yu* (also known as *feng shui*). Concepts of *feng shui* and *qi* (energy) have been applied in the zoning, planning and construction of buildings and interior design, with the intention to create environments that best conform to nature and suit human habitation.

According to ancient Chinese sages, literature should be a vehicle for propagating the *Tao* or the true way. Any system or school of thought that consists of the description, elaboration and espousal of the *Tao* is identified by it. To capture the cultural values and essential thinking of that system, an interior designer avails herself of every means at her disposal to create an interior space that conforms to the *Tao* advocated by that particular school of thought. It is in this sense that interior design serves as a vehicle for the *Tao*.

On facing page You may wonder about the rationale behind this design with a pair of over-sized birdcages set against crude-looking materials and furniture? The answer lies perhaps in the green pine on the table.

Confucianism—
"Confucian-elegant" Spaces

A Chinese author relates in her book a critical remark made by her German landlord about the smile worn by many Chinese as they greet people. It seemed to him as if they were always getting ready to ask a favor. But you can attribute it to their good upbringing if you look at it from a different angle. Traditional Chinese upbringing has its roots and basis in Confucianism, founded by Confucius in the Spring and Autumn period (770 – 476 BC). Adopted as an official ideology for thousands of years, it has profoundly influenced China and has become a cornerstone of Chinese civilization. It may well be that most Chinese can't give a coherent account of Confucianism but *ren yi li zhi xin*, the Confucian concepts of humanity, righteousness, rituals, knowledge and

A small decorative object, with its symmetrical form, muted color tone and natural material, projects a sense of *li*, i.e. order, prized by traditional Chinese culture.

trustworthiness, have been burned into the national ethos, so much so that to this day they still base their judgment on these subconscious criteria and standards—as in the interpretation of the "smile" mentioned above. *Ren*, or humanity, is the core of Confucian thinking. Confucius elevated it to the highest moral principle, standard and ideal. *Ren* means *ai ren*, or love for others; it is love based on doing unto others as you would have them do unto you. It is in the broadest sense love for humanity, manifested in sympathy, care, tolerance, pity and charity. *Li*, or ritual, is another important concept of Confucianism. *Ke ji fu li*, or restraining one's desires and respecting norms and rituals, is a means of achieving *ren*. To put it simply, *ren* is good-heartedness that conforms to social norms and rituals. A good-hearted person that respects social norms and rituals is likely to have a cheerful

and pleasant demeanor.

Cultural vehicles, such as music, painting, literature and other art forms, reflect or embody some cultural values or currents of thought. The same is true for traditional Chinese interior decoration and design. In contrast to other art forms, interior design is not the preserve of the highbrowed or cultured lot; rather, it is a way of living accessible to ordinary people. It more directly reflects their way of life and offers a clearer insight into their aesthetic tastes and the intellectual and moral tendencies driving them. In planning and arranging their living spaces, people either leave unintentional clues of the influence of some current of thought, or design their living space expressly to make a statement about their aspirations and world outlook. Since Confucianism has a more popular following compared to Taoism

A symmetrical placement of furniture centered on a round mural painting in a square interior space is a classical technique used to create a Confucian-inspired space.

and Buddhism, a larger part of traditional Chinese interior design has been devoted to creating spaces that are "Confucian-elegant" in form, space planning and technique as a reflection of the impact of Confucianism.

Square Shape   From the street grid of a city down to the shape and form of an individual home, the most orthodox design in China is unquestionably the "square shape." Whether in the courtyard house (*si he yuan*) that is popular in the north or the pavilions in the classical gardens of the south, whether in the elegant and stately Forbidden City or in the civilian dwellings and compounds tucked away in narrow streets (*hu tong*) and alleys, the prevalent form of traditional architecture and interior spaces is the square. Even doors, windows, beds, tables and utensils are mostly square-shaped. The square shape is favored for its excellent functionality, but more importantly, it is often associated with desirable human qualities.

If we compare geometrical shapes to people, then the square shape would possess a solid,

impartial and honest personality; if shapes were to represent the qualities prized by Confucianism, then righteousness, loyalty, trustworthiness, down-to-earth simplicity, unbending probity and integrity are all squares. The Chinese often refer to a Confucian gentleman as *fang zheng ru ya*, or a square and upright, urbane Confucian scholar. An honest official is said to be *fang zheng qing lian*, or square and upright, and clean. Someone on a just mission is *fang zheng bu e*, or square and upright, and uncompromising. Obviously *fang zheng*, or being square and upright, is in the Chinese mind one of the most desirable qualities. *Fang zheng* also conveys an impression of old-fashioned seriousness, restraint and conformity, but these can be likened to the strict Confucian requirements of uprightness, prudence, self-discipline and propriety in thinking and conduct.

Therefore, in traditional Chinese interior design, interior spaces and objects are often square-shaped; lines in furnishings and space composition are often rectilinear, and simplicity is emphasized in the techniques of mixing materials and colors and the logical relationship between

This is an interesting encounter of tradition and modernity—patently classical calligraphy scrolls deliberately hung in an asymmetrical fashion to highlight a modernist freedom of spirit; and the bright red and green colors of the clearly Western-style candles add a Chinese element.

Furniture and furnishings arranged in axial symmetry and space divided by the use of screens embody the Confucian concept of *li*, or conformity to norms and rituals, with a symmetrical and well-ordered design.

spaces. This design approach that most conforms to orthodoxy and tradition seems more amenable to the creation of spaces of distinct personalities—bright and orthodox for the powerful political class; magnificent and opulent for the rich merchant class; sober and restrained for the literati, and peaceful, comfortable for the common folks. Highbrow or lowbrow, elegant or plain, a space with a "square" personality tends to conjure a positive, noble image and symbolism. It coincides with the aesthetic tastes and standards ingrained in them by Confucianism, or traditional education. It reflects conventional wisdom.

Symmetry   A survey of traditional Chinese designs shows that symmetrical arrangement is a major shared feature: palaces and houses in axial symmetry, Chinese-style halls with symmetrically placed furniture and decorative objects, structural and decorative symmetry, symmetrically placed vases, vertical couplets (*dui lian*) and door-guarding stone beasts. One possible explanation for the Chinese fascination with symmetrical beauty is its symbolism of happy union, even-handedness, impartiality, harmony and perfection. But in the final analysis this preference for symmetry probably has its intellectual parentage in the Chinese identification with and high regard for Confucianism.

Confucianism places a high premium on *li*, or respect for norms and rituals. To put it simply, *li* is a system of moral norms and codes of conduct. One of its commandments is *jun jun chen chen, fu fu zi zi*, or the sovereign should behave like a sovereign, the subject like a subject, the father should behave like a father, the son like a son.

Confucian theory holds that so long as every member of society observes its norms, its rules of conduct and the social order, with each knowing one's place and behaving as it befits his station, stability and harmony will reign in society. While it is true that seen from a modern perspective, "feudal Confucian ethics" played the role of a straitjacket on people's thinking and behavior and acted as a brake on societal progress and development, Confucian ethics did offer a code of social conduct designed to maintain normal social intercourse and a stable social framework. Therefore, it undeniably played an important part in the spiritual development of the Chinese people.

"Symmetry" is a design concept that captures the spirit of Confucian ethics. Its approach to space arrangement is aimed at creating a state of absolute balance in which everything falls in its place. It projects a sense of orthodoxy, rationality, stability and permanence and its beauty lies in its conformity to the Confucian code of conduct. Like the previously discussed "square shape," it also captures the essence of Confucianism in the sense that, in form and in personality, it projects an image of propriety and rigorous adherence to rules.

Therefore, symmetry is essential to the creation of a space that evokes the essence of Chinese design and also one of the easiest and most effective ways to accomplish it. Symmetry can be embodied in space arrangement, in the placement of furniture and in the choice of furnishings. A table and two chairs arranged symmetrically in a corner of a room, accented by a traditional Chinese painting hung in the middle,

Symmetry implies union and harmony. Stone, the dominant material here, symbolizes, with its characteristic hardness and regular shape, the Confucian gentleman's honesty and probity.

could instantly create a rich Chinese effect.

Order   *Li* (respect for norms and rituals) is the core and the foundation of the traditional Chinese ethical order. The system followed by traditional Chinese architecture and interior design, which is deeply rooted in society's hierarchical order and code of social conduct, corresponds to the pedagogical vocation of Confucian ethics. A case in point is the courtyard house: principal structures such as the main hall and rooms housing the elders are located on the central axis while structures of lesser rank are built on secondary axes. The arrangement of courtyards and rooms follows an ethical hierarchy based on principles such as

"private facilities come after public ones," "anterior buildings must not be higher than posterior ones" and "side structures must not be higher than central ones" and differentiation according to social standing, age, gender and blood relationship.

Therefore the creation of order in spatial arrangement, like the use of symmetry as a design tool, is an approach that follows Confucian doctrine. In the arrangement of interior space as well, traditional Chinese design often uses partitions and screens to divide it into principal and secondary, anterior and posterior subspaces. Furniture, such as Chinese-style alcove beds or bookshelves, can also play a role in the further ordering of a space.

The famous verse "*ting yuan shen shen shen ji xu*" ("Deep in the walled garden, deep—how deep?") describes a traditional Chinese residence composed of multiple courtyards, each one further in from the street. In the process of building a multi-courtyard residence to satisfy the need for order, traditional Chinese architecture also created a sense of mystery and charm associated with the spatial depth.

Proportions   The *Treatise on Architectural Methods* (*Ying Zao Fa Shi*), a book published in the Song dynasty (960 – 1279) that has since greatly influenced traditional Chinese architecture, gave detailed descriptions of building forms, materials and construction methods, and set out clear specifications for the dimensions and proportions of all styles of buildings, architectural and decorative components. There was, in fact, a complete system of rules and regulations in traditional Chinese building codes covering the measurements of structures of different rankings, the corresponding grades of materials, the number of tiers of timber bracketing and roof shapes and the measurements of decorative details. It was a system that reflected the influence of Confucian tradition on architecture and interior design and the measures taken in response to that influence.

Proportions are an important consideration in traditional Chinese interior design, both in terms of scale and dimensions and in the ranking of the building in question. In other words you'll never find in traditional Chinese interior designs any disproportion between furniture and space, nor violations of the proper rankings, such as the use of hip roofs or other construction components and decorative elements reserved for higher-ranking buildings in the construction of civilian housing.

Therefore, the use of proper scale and proportion is critical to the creation of a traditional Chinese-style interior, both as an architectural and design requirement and as a reflection of traditional ideology. Even without the use of any

distinctly Chinese decorative elements, appropriate proportion can still give an interior space a rich classically traditional Chinese cachet. Alternatively, there is a post-modern technique in interior decoration inspired by contemporary design thinking that consists of accenting an interior space with Chinese furniture of exaggerated proportions or stylized decorative elements.

These are some of the commonly used techniques and important considerations in traditional Chinese interior design. Their application in Chinese interior design reflects the profound impact of Confucianism. To echo the values of traditional aesthetics, the Chinese have promoted a concept of beauty based on moderation and harmony (*zhong he*) in all art forms, including interior design. It is a concept that conforms to Confucian thinking.

Moderation and harmony marry Confucian values and Confucian methodology. *Zhong* (moderation or the middle way) represents a fundamental Chinese way of thinking. Taking the middle way helps ease tensions and improve living conditions. *He* (harmony) can be said to be a cardinal credo of Chinese civilization; it stands for harmony, coordination, balance, order, collaboration and cooperation. In the Confucian system of thinking, harmony represents the optimal scheme of things. Traditional Chinese interior design strives for this beauty of harmony by using the square shape, symmetry and appropriate proportions and rankings. But it is possible to totally disregard these set rules and formulas, and still preserve the essence of traditional Chinese culture in the design, as long as it lives up to the artistic ideal of *zhong he*.

The axial symmetry in this design gives a sense of orthodox beauty. The spatial depth reflects Confucian values such as social hierarchy and order.

Taoism—The *Tao* of Heaven Lets Nature Be

Taoism, represented by Laozi (also known as Lao Tzu) and Zhuangzi (also known as Chuang Tzu), is one of the most important schools of thought that flourished in China's Spring and Autumn period (770 – 476 BC) and the Warring States period (475 – 221 BC). It explains the world's origin, noumenon, laws and principles with the philosophical category of the *Tao*. The main thinking of Taoism can be summarized as respecting the *Tao* and letting nature be with minimal interference. While it is true that of the three pillars of traditional Chinese philosophy, Confucianism has had a more profound influence on Chinese thought than Buddhism and Taoism, but Taoism has undoubtedly left the deepest imprint on traditional Chinese art.

The perception of aesthetics in traditional Chinese culture has been profoundly influenced by the Taoist belief that "the *Tao* is beauty" and "emptiness is beauty." To see beauty in the *Tao*, one looks for a "realm beyond appearance" and

"poetry beyond lyric." It is a quest for a "landscape of the mind" that transcends physical existence and appearance. The beauty of emptiness is mainly reflected in the traditional Chinese aesthetic principle of "synergy between presence and absence," which strives to create a mood of emptiness and blankness. Another Taoist-inspired concept in traditional Chinese art is beauty that cannot be expressed in words or seen in sharp focus and beauty that comes from the harmonious union of opposites. In traditional Chinese art the best works are those that appear to be wrought by nature, simple and plain, because in Taoist belief *tian dao* (the *Tao* or Way of Heaven) always lets nature be. The Taoist concepts of union of man and nature (*tian ren he yi*) and emulation of nature (*shi fa zi ran*) have had considerable impact on the cultivation of aesthetic awareness, artistic creation and artistic techniques in China.

Specifically, the influence of Taoist thinking on Chinese architecture and interior design is

Simple, natural materials, colors, and forms expressing the Taoist idea of "purity and do-nothingness" give the space an air of calm and peace.

A stark and simple design style is itself a reflection of Taoist thinking. These unique furnishings are the finishing touches that bring the décor to life.

mainly manifested in the adherence to the Taoist concepts of "union of man and nature," "emulation of nature," "synergy between presence and absence" and "inner serenity and do-nothingness" in exterior and interior space planning, the creation of architectural spaces, the selection of building materials and the creation of interior ambiance.

Union of Man and Nature (*Tian Ren He Yi*)

Tian means nature. In Taoist belief humankind is a part of nature and there are commonalities and similarities between man and nature. It emphasizes the importance of letting nature be and following the laws of nature, and calls for the harmonious coexistence of man and nature. As applied to traditional architecture and design this belief advocates the harmonious union of man and the architectural environment, and of architecture and the exterior environment.

Under Taoist influence, traditional Chinese architecture and interior design exalt nature, emulate nature and seek to preserve nature. One way to preserve nature is for builders of houses and gardens to try as much as possible to keep changes to the natural environment to a minimum. This is done mainly by adapting the construction, e.g. site selection, to the environment and landscaping that takes advantage of the natural

If the bonsai in this photo represents a straight-forward example of nature, then the entire space constituted by the windows made of wood, drum stools made of stone, and a floor paved with brick tiles, all materials taken from nature and retaining their original colors, epitomizes a subtle, unspoken, but persistent effort to create a natural, unadorned ambiance.

features of the site. A second way is to follow the laws of nature and to learn from the workings of nature in the design and creative process, making sure, for example, that space arrangement, forms and shapes are natural and offer a sensation of flow, and proportions and dimensions are on a human-friendly scale. A third way is to endeavor to create a back-to-basics, back-to-nature ambiance in which man-made structures blend inconspicuously into nature and have the look and feel of being part of nature.

Creating an appropriate structure that adapts to the features of the natural environment is another way to achieve the "union of man and nature." In rain-rich south China, traditional architecture favors sloped roofs; in arid north China flat roofs are a more common sight. In humid southeast China, where reptiles are a concern, stilt houses are preferred. In frigid northeast China, people have adopted more of the local flavor in their furniture and accessories, such as a raised platform heated from below (*huo kang*). Another

way of achieving the "union of man and nature" in interior design and decoration is to take into account the inhabitants' biological needs and daily habits when designing functionality, and reflect the resident's personality and tastes in choosing furnishings and styles.

Local sourcing is the most common example of applying the concept of the "union of man and nature" to the selection of building materials. The materials most often used in traditional Chinese architecture and interior decoration are wood, bamboo and stone. The application of the concept of round heaven and square earth (*tian yuan di fang*) in the determination of architectural forms and space planning is a response to the union between man and nature in the creation of a desired ambiance. Another application of the concept of the "union between man and nature" is the creation of a poetic, visually appealing ambiance in architectural and interior design to produce a positive resonance between the viewer and the environment.

Emulation of Nature   "Man takes his law from the Earth; the Earth takes its law from Heaven; Heaven takes its law from the *Dao*. The law of the *Dao* is its being what it is," writes Laozi (Translation of James Legge). In Taoist theory there is an internal law governing man, the universe and nature. Humankind should, therefore, find and identify this law from the workings of the universe and nature, and learn from it. In the case of architecture, traditional design often discovers beauty in nature and draws inspirations from it before implementing them in its aesthetic choices, ambiance creation and design techniques.

Traditional Chinese architecture and interior design attach great importance to the creation of beauty that is inspired by and emulates nature, as shown in the simplicity of design, streamlined forms, soft colors and the use of simple materials drawn from it.

In the creation of a natural ambiance, designers often seek to add a touch of nature to the interior by way of space arrangement and the selection of proper materials and decorative accessories. For example, when furnishing a study in a traditional house, a freer, more casual arrangement of furniture, or a furniture ensemble including a "natural desk" in the form of a root, can create a mini-environment in which the occupant can temporarily forget the stresses and hassle of the daily routine. A popular design technique is the massive use of bamboo or natural wood to accentuate the sense of nature of the room. Decorative objects often used to add a touch of nature to a room include potted landscapes, flower arrangements and rockeries. Walled gardens and

interior spaces are closely interrelated in traditional Chinese architecture, and live plants, mounds, ponds and other scenic elements are organized in a natural-looking way around the buildings to create a man-made landscape that betrays few traces of the hand of man. Unlike European gardens, traditional Chinese gardens do not feature topiaries in geometric shapes or symmetrical patterns. On the contrary, every thought is given to the placement of every plant and every stone in such a way that the man-made environment will resemble the wilderness.

The interior space and the architectural structure are closely linked in traditional Chinese architecture. The architectural structure is also inspired by the concepts of emulating and adapting to nature—the timber used in wooden structural members is usually flexible and mortise, and tendon joints are widely used between members so that there is room to stretch and rotate like in human joints. This design enables the building to absorb and dissipate seismic energy through internal flexing in an earthquake, minimizing the danger of building collapse. Another instance of nature emulation can be found in the ergonomic designs of *quan yi*, or the armchair with curved

rest, and the master armchair with its curved back (*tai shi yi*), two notable examples of Ming-style furniture.

Synergy between Presence and Absence

A Chinese painting showing a fish bursting with life in a totally blank setting can strike the viewer as brimming with water. This is an example of traditional Chinese art demonstrating what's present can evoke what's absent and vice versa; and the visible can be absent and the invisible can be present. *Liu bai*, or the intentional leaving of blank spaces in art works, is a very important technique in traditional Chinese art. Chinese artists believe that what is left unsaid is more important than what is said. An "invisible" space evoked and opened up by something "visible" leaves ample room for imagination. It is one of the wonderful effects of art. One may say that the ability to work with both the present and visible and the absent and invisible is essential for achieving an artistic effect and mood that is distinctly Chinese; and the unity of the opposites of the present and the absent is the dialectics of Chinese art.

In traditional Chinese architecture and interior design, as in other traditional art forms, the synergy of presence and absence is a popular

Chinese garden designs seek to create a dynamic, lively, and wild-looking mini-environment to emulate nature.

The white wall serves to highlight the exquisite carving work. The two stems of bamboo against the texture of the wall evoke the picture of a grove of bamboo in the wild.

and ingenious design technique. The architectural form integrating courtyards and living quarters is itself a reflection of this synergy: the courtyard may appear to be an unenclosed outdoor space, but when it is surrounded by living quarters, it becomes part of the building complex. In the same vein a window is an "absence" relative to the interior space, but it can usher in the scenery of the garden, which is a "presence," and blend it into the ambiance of the interior, producing a decorative effect. In traditional interior design, openwork partitions, lattices, sheer screens or other half "absent" partitions are often used to subdivide a room, creating a fluid, dynamic configuration of spaces that seems unable to decide whether they are separated or connected. White interior walls are often used to set off the darker-toned, beautifully grained and finely crafted furniture and

woodwork so that the craftsmanship will come to the fore. This is another example of using *liu bai* to create an artistic effect. Traditional Chinese interior decoration features horizontal inscribed tablets and vertical couplets that often become the soul of the room although they usually consist of a few characters or lines only. The profound wisdom of the words inspires the viewer to look with fresh eyes at the aesthetics of the exterior and interior spaces, opening a vista beyond the actual scene and transforming a physical scene into an intellectual vision.

Inner Serenity and Do-nothingness

In Taoist theory *wu wei* (doing nothing) is simply following the laws of nature, and is therefore more powerful than *you wei* (undertaking some kind of intervention). The Taoist view of aesthetics is reflected in statements such as "simplicity is the best choice" and "crude appearance often belies great refinement." In other words, things preserved in their original, native state are the most beautiful. Artistic creation should also strive for unadorned simplicity and show as little hand of man as possible. As discussed above, traditional Chinese architecture and interior design place a high premium on following the laws of nature and creating a natural beauty and ambiance.

Inner serenity and do-nothingness, as a philosophical concept, has also deeply influenced people's thought, conduct, character and aspirations. Therefore, in traditional architecture and interior decoration one often finds the use of a spartan arrangement of spaces, simple lines and furniture, and clean colors to create an ambiance that soothes body and mind, because people associate them with Taoist ideas such as "inner serenity enables one to go far and absence of greed firms one's resolve."

In sum, traditional Chinese architecture and interior design, like other traditional art forms, emulate, borrow ideas from and interact with nature in their aesthetic choices, creation of ambiance and in creative and execution techniques. It is in fact a quest for the *Tao*—both the "artistic *Tao*" of interior design and the "*Tao* of Heaven" of the universe and nature. This is where the essence and the artistic spirit of traditional Chinese design lie.

Buddhism—
Transcending the Earthly World

Buddhism is one of the three pillars of traditional Chinese culture. Unlike the other two schools of thought, Buddhism did not originate in China but was brought into China from India in the Han dynasty (206 BC – 220 AD). After centuries of evolution Buddhism became simplified with the incorporation of elements of Confucian ethics and Taoist concepts such as "the *Tao* of Heaven lets nature be." In its Chinese version, Buddhism replaces its proscriptions with rules of conduct in an effort to adapt to Chinese moral life; it shifts its focus from the meditative practice of India to intellectual enlightenment in a nod to the Taoist idea of "following the laws of nature." In the late Tang dynasty, Chan (later translated by the Japanese as Zen) Buddhism almost replaced

With the wall featuring a relief carving of the Buddha and Buddhist text as a background, will the admirer of the potted plants have a better understanding of the feeling of the Buddha with a smile on his face and a flower in his hand?

The ancient statue of Buddha and the classical furniture share a common decorative style. The Buddha in the room and the green bamboo outside the window create a resonant link between the interior and the exterior.

other school, and Chan became the synonym of Buddhism.

The Chinese Chan school of Buddhist thought advocates a theory of *xin xing* (the self-existing fundamental pure mind), believing that once one "beholds the Buddha-nature within oneself" one will "awaken to the truth." The Chan school believes that the fundamental, original human mind is pure, but it has been obscured by man's obsession with vanities and illusions. Awakening comes only by reacquainting oneself with one's original purity through "Prajñā." Chan offers a way to attain the wisdom of "Prajñā" through "dhyāna," which enables one to "behold the Buddha-nature within oneself."

For thousands of years Chan thinking has

not only had a profound influence on traditional Chinese culture but has made itself felt in every aspect of life, creating a body of practical wisdom accessible to ordinary people. The fact that the Chan (Zen) style has retained a presence among the various schools and styles of interior design in China and even in Southeast Asia is a testimony to the important impact of Chan Buddhism.

Zen style designs aim at the creation of a space to make a statement about the resident's determination to shed worldly concerns and gain enlightenment, and to inspire visitors. Some of the important features of Zen interior design are explained below.

A Stark Style   Chan Buddhism aspires to soar above the earthly world, to achieve a state of *kong ji* far removed from everything of this world. In Buddhism, *kong ji* is an ability to feel quiet and undisturbed even amid noise and bustle—a strong inner serenity. *Kong ji* is a condition beyond disturbance. It represents peace of mind and serenity, and is different from lifeless silent solitude. In art, *kong ji* often expresses itself in spareness or emptiness. In Zen style décors there is a purity and simplicity that dispense with unnecessary lines and ornamentation; the room may even appear quite empty, an emptiness that precisely embodies the Chan concept of "all is void." A neat and clean space is relaxing and contributes to one's peace of mind and inner tranquility; it also symbolizes the resident's "spotless state of mind."

Zen designs are stark but not crude. In fact they put a lot of thought into details such as in the selection and use of the texture and grain of materials and lighting effects to best advantage. Care goes into as small a detail as a flower arrangement—a vase may hold only a single fresh-cut flower but the classic elegance of the vase and ingenious lighting can accentuate the freshness of the flower and bring the dew drops on the petals into relief. One may say that the general simplicity of the décor focuses more sharply the mind on the single flower to discover the universality of truth and to realize the link between the moment and eternity when one waits patiently for a dew drop to roll off a petal.

Muted colors   The first step for a Buddhist is to cultivate purity of mind. Only by keeping one's mind pure can one have the great wisdom to have a true understanding of the world and shed one's obsessions and troubles. In the same vein, Chan-style design also seeks purity in interior spaces, mainly by the use of simple coordinated colors and muted natural tones.

Zen designers, who are believers in emulating nature, use mostly colors taken from it, such as milk white, off-white, beige and brown. In interior design, they minimize the number of colors used and coordinate the colors of walls, furniture and fabrics to achieve a general effect of simplicity. In keeping with the Buddhist admonition of maintaining a "tranquil frame of mind," they also choose colors that do not clash or stand in sharp contrast. In order to preserve the beautiful colors and the grain of the materials, fine clear paint is preferred over regular paint for decorative and protective purposes.

Clean Lines   A stark Zen style means Zen designers prefer clean, simple lines—mostly straight with occasional curves, not for an ornamental effect, but to capture a natural shape. Sometimes less is more. Zen designers use a no

Like the beam of light shone on the inscriptions on the stone tablet, Buddhist thinking has become a beacon of wisdom and civilization.

decorative technique to restore things to their original purity and to achieve beauty in something that is plain and simple.

The clean simple lines favored by Zen designers, often reflected in small dimensions, square shapes and eschewal of complexities, are expressive of the resident's forthright and sincere temperament. Simple lines in furniture, as reflected in an unadorned look and low profiles, are used to match the resident's amicable nature and frugality. Accessories with simple lines, reflected in a quaint elegance, highlight the resident's unconventional grace and taste. The use of simple unadorned patterns is favored for the interior and exterior trims of doors and windows, and for the moldings and grilles of sliding doors to match the general décor.

Natural Materials   As mentioned above, Zen decorators favor natural materials, the inherent texture and grain for which they find beautiful, and love to highlight. Stone, wood, rattan, grasses, and other natural materials are common in Japanese-style décors. They are used in the manufacture of furniture and wood trims, and some form part of the building structure. The furniture and decorative woodwork made from these materials may be simple in form and appearance, and mainly serve a functional purpose, but the beauty of their natural texture shines through because of careful selection and fine manufacturing. Thus, the resulting decorative effect is of a refreshing elegance that helps one relax and escape the daily hustle and bustle. It also embodies the Buddhist concept of *sama* equality by showing respect for all beings and things in the world, even if it is only a tree or a stand of bamboo, and by bowing in awe and humbleness before nature.

One can imagine oneself surrounded by nature, relaxed and free from all care and hassle when one enters such a décor evocative of the fresh scent of soil! One comes to see the magnificence of nature and the insignificance of our human person, and is moved to reexamine the meaning and value of life. One can then feel a step closer to Śākyamuni Buddha, who attained enlightenment underneath a bodhi tree.

Light Decorative Touches   For Zen design, one finds decorative accessories with lasting appeal and interesting metaphorical and symbolic meanings. Sometimes a couple of graphic patterns or objects with a Buddhist theme can instantly infuse a plain dull space with a Zen aura and bring out a sense of simple profundity. For example, a few stems of lotus flowers, considered sacred in Buddhism, placed at an angle in a simple and primitive-looking vase will be a quiet statement about the resident's unworldly refinement. A stone Buddha strikes a chord with its rough texture, muted color tone, and simple crude form. A close study of its serene sitting posture and facial expression induces an inner calm. It is well known that tea and Chan are closely associated with each other in China and other countries of Asia. Therefore, a hand-made pottery tea set can evoke Chan stories and anecdotes. A primitive-looking oil lamp reminds one that Buddhist wisdom, like a beacon in the darkness, dispels ignorance.

It is important to know that what counts in Zen accessories is quality over quantity, inner beauty instead of a flashy exterior. This is dictated by the understatement and restraint of the Zen style. Just as Buddha's smile and the flower held in his hand convey a serene and peaceful positive mind-state, ornaments to enliven a room of simple elegance should also offer aesthetic enjoyment, intellectual enlightenment, and spiritual elevation.

If we only look at their impact on interior decoration, Taoist and Buddhist manifestations may appear to be similar or even overlap in that they both see beauty in *kong* (emptiness) and seek to create a calming and peaceful ambiance using simple forms, muted colors, and natural materials in decoration. But behind this surface similarity the two schools of thought differ in intellectual content and origin, with Taoism seeking to accomplish its goals in this world by "escaping this world." In Taoism, *kong* (emptiness) leads to fulfillment and the result of *wu wei* (do nothing) is *wu suo bu wei* (everything is done). Following the laws of nature is for the purpose of living to a ripe old age. However, Buddhism believes in "leaving this world" spiritually by truly understanding and transcending life and death, even though pious Buddhists are seen to actively engage in worldly affairs, appearing to be "of this world." In short, Taoism seeks a mental and emotional emptiness while Buddhism seeks a spiritual and true emptiness.

On facing page With the sitting Buddha, this décor composed of natural wood and muted colors is able to transcend its simplicity and exude an inspiring calm.

Feng Shui—
The Realm of Good Auspices

Kan yu, also known as *feng shui*, is an ancient Chinese system of methods and principles used to select auspicious locations for buildings, including palaces, settlements, and tombs. *Kan* means heaven and *yu* means earth; and *kan yu* is a study or science of heaven and earth. Its theory is based on the ancient *River Chart* (*He Tu*) and *Book from the River Luo* (*Luo Shu*), combined with the principles of the Eight Trigrams (*ba gua*), the Nine Stars (*jiu xing*), *yin* and *yang* (male and female), and the mutual promotion, repulsion and influence of the Five Elements (*wu xing*). It is a theoretical system incorporating the *Tao* of heaven, the flow of the *qi* (energy) of earth, and man (between heaven and earth), to assess or alter fortunes and misfortunes. In ancient times, the Chinese believed that *kan yu* was closely bound up with one's fortunes.

In fact, *kan yu* was originally intended to help select auspicious locations only. That it has come to be known also as *feng shui* points up the importance of wind (*feng*) and water (*shui*) in the theory of *kan yu*. The study of wind and water can, in a way, find a basis in modern science in that the construction of dwellings should meet the objective requirements of human habitation in terms of health and comfort.

The theory of *kan yu* has numerous uses in traditional architecture, from site selection to the general architectural plan and form of the building, and the shapes and orientations of the individual rooms. In interior design, *kan yu* is used mainly in the general management of the interior space, the treatment of special structural components, the selection and matching of colors, and the use of auspicious ornaments and accessories. As times change and science advances, the superstitious ideas of *feng shui* have gradually been debunked and abandoned. But some scientific aspects of *feng shui* have suffered collateral damage and undeserved neglect in the process of change. This is indeed a loss for China's cultural heritage. It is my hope that through its analysis of traditional Chinese interior design and its findings this book

This auspicious relief carving features a sword, a flower basket, and the other ritual pieces attributed to the Eight Immortals that supposedly possess magical, mystical powers, reflects the wish to ward off evil spirits and bring in good luck.

will help more people understand the relevance of certain aspects of *kan yu*.

Space Management   While the modern trend is for greater specialization, there is a high degree of integration between traditional Chinese architecture and interior design. Thus, *kan yu*'s management of interior spaces is largely accomplished already in the architectural planning stage to determine the configuration of the rooms, the relative positioning of the rooms, the orientations of the principal rooms, and the positioning of special-purpose rooms. Some of the

ideas of *kan yu* have rational explanations. For example, the street door of traditional Chinese houses usually faces south to benefit from more natural light and to facilitate ventilation. *Feng shui* advises against having a street directly running toward the front door because of safety concerns and the annoyance factor of a noisy environment. The rule against having one's front door face a toilet facility or other unclean installations is justifiable from a sanitary and psychological point of view. While people nowadays are obsessed with spacious rooms, traditional architecture determines the size of a room more in light of its function.

According to folklore, ghosts walk in a straight line, so people began to erect the screen wall near the entry gate (*zhao bi*) to ward off evil spirits. The stone carvings of phoenixes, peonies, the animals carved on embracing drum (*bao gu shi*), and patterns of flowers and plants above the door are all auspicious symbols intended to bring good luck.

The canopy bed (*jia zi chuang*) enclosed in draperies creates a cozy nook where one enjoys quiet, a greater sense of security, and relaxation of body and mind. The red color of the wall adds warmth and a sense of "home" to an interior of simple, subdued colors.

Feng shui believes that over-sized bedrooms are undesirable because they tend to absorb or dampen human *qi* (energy). From a scientific viewpoint, cavernous bedrooms make people feel cold, lonely, and exposed. It may even induce fear, which is not good for rest and relaxation. For this reason, over-sized bedrooms are rare in traditional Chinese homes, or in royal palaces for that matter; they are usually a space measuring less than 20 square meters and closed off by an openwork partition. Furthermore, the hardwood canopy beds with curtains found in traditional bedrooms are like rooms unto themselves, adding to the coziness and sense of security.

Modern interior design is often done post-construction and is therefore prevented from any major rearrangement of rooms. Designers can

in such circumstances only make adjustments within limits and use design techniques to remedy deficiencies in *feng shui*. When the apartment door is directly opposite a bathroom or a bedroom, partitions or green plants are placed in the foyer to block intrusive eyes and to avoid the awkward public display of intimate activities. A heightened red tone in north-facing rooms relieves the sense of sunless cold by giving visual warmth.

Details   Traditional Chinese interior design pays particular attention to the entry door, the stove, the toilet facility, and structural members such as beams and pillars in the belief that they have an important bearing on the *feng shui* of the entire building. The stove, for example, is considered in *feng shui* to be pivotal to the financial well-being of a home, and therefore the wealth of

Like stone lions commonly found outside the entry door of traditional buildings, this pair of decorative lions—one cradling a cub lion and the other toying with a embroidered ball (*xiu qiu*)—symbolizes a wish for many children and peace in the family. The potted pine, a symbol of longevity, adds to the good luck.

the homeowner. For this reason the stove in a household should not face the entry door, the master bedroom door, or the door of the toilet room; nor should it be too close to anything having to do with water (*shui*), such as sinks and washing machines. This rule actually arose from a concern to make sure the stove fire is not extinguished by drafts, doused by water, or polluted by impurities. The stove, or the kitchen, is after all the center of food preparation in a home and is essential for keeping the family well-fed and in good health. Therefore, this focus on the stove translates to

The stone screen directly in front of the entry door plays the role of a screen wall in *feng shui*. The pond planted with *he hua* (lotus) is supposed to bring wealth (in Chinese *feng shui* water is associated with wealth) and to bring harmony, because a homonym of the flower *he* is harmony.

a concern for the health and wellbeing of the family. With good health, the family members can go out and make money. Another example is an exposed beam in a house, which is considered bad for *feng shui*, and the negative energy of this "overbearing beam" needs to be dissipated in some manner. This may sound like nonsense, but if sofas, desks, beds, and other pieces of furniture of frequent use are placed directly beneath a beam, people will subconsciously feel oppressed and may eventually develop fatigue and a rigid neck or discomfort in other parts of the body. This problem is often solved by the use of suspended ceilings. Columns are another concern of *feng shui*. Mystic considerations apart, columns do block the view and people do bump into them. To fix this problem designers often place bookcases, wine cabinets, and ornamental lattice partitions in the space between a column and the wall.

Selection of Colors Research reveals that colors affect human biological functions. Certain combinations of colors can bring well-being to body and mind, add enjoyment to life, and raise work efficiency while other color combinations may create the opposite effects. There are rules about color use for buildings in China's *feng shui* system. It explains why certain colors are suitable for certain orientations and locations on the basis of the theories of *yin* and *yang* and the Five Elements. For example, south is associated with the element of fire, which corresponds to the colors of red or purple. The rules of the Five Elements say that water overwhelms fire. Accordingly, colors that represent water, such as black and blue, are inappropriate for south-facing rooms.

From the standpoint of color psychology, lighter and warmer colors are more suitable for living quarters. Strong colors may be good for creating eye-catching mass visual effects, but long exposure to such an environment could produce extreme moods such as exasperation, excitability, and irascibility. Colder color tones could induce loneliness and boredom or even make occupants feel physically cold. Therefore, colors closer to nature such as cream, beige, and natural wood tones are best for human habitats and interior decoration. Harmony and compatibility between the interior surfaces are important considerations. For example, a lighter color for the ceiling relative to the walls and the floor conforms to the *feng shui* concept of "clear heaven and turbid earth," and is less likely to produce an unwelcome feeling of top-heaviness and oppression.

Use of Decorative Accessories A close examination of ornamental objects used in traditional Chinese interior design reveals that many of them have an auspicious symbolic meaning. Special rules have been made for the placement of these objects. As mentioned above, interior design is often done in the framework of the architectural plan. When the interior designers have to work under the assumption that no major structural modifications are allowed, they often resort to the use of ornamental objects to meet *feng shui* requirements. The placement of a potted green plant at an entry door deemed to have bad *feng shui* will not only effectively shield the house from prying eyes and divert unwelcome curiosity, but also create a visually appealing sight. Other examples are the placement of a *hua ping* (flower vase), which shares a homophone with *ping an* (safe and sound), auspicious symbols such as a Buddhist rosary, a statue of Buddha or a *feng shui* wheel, and paintings and calligraphy scrolls with a well-meaning message, for the soothing effect of subtle psychological suggestion, a positive mood change, renewed energy, and enhanced mental wellbeing.

However, not all ornaments are good for *feng shui*. The hanging of paintings with a forlorn theme or wild beasts and fowl is likely to have a creeping negative psychological impact. It is not a good idea to hang a mirror at the head of a bed, because one may be spooked by what one sees reflected in the mirror in a half-awake state and the mirror may cause a nervousness that keeps one awake. Needle-bearing plants and plants that wilt easily should be avoided as indoor decoration because they might cause accidental injury or have a negative psychological impact.

Superstitious elements in the age-old practice of *feng shui* have been debunked as science and human knowledge progress. But one falls prey to another kind of superstition if one considers anything outside of what is already known today as unscientific. Although modern science cannot as yet offer any conclusive explanation of the theories of *yin* and *yang*, the Five Elements, the Eight Trigrams and the Nine Stars, these theories are not without merit given their psychological and subliminal impact on people. *Feng shui* ideas that have been validated by modern science are further proof that its ancient wisdom is still relevant today.

Chapter 2
Traditional Chinese Art
in Chinese Interior Design

Confucius exhorts: "Swim in the Arts," meaning a Confucian scholar, after receiving a comprehensive education, should become an expert swimmer in the sea of the six arts of "rites, music, archery, chariot-driving, reading, and mathematics." Today, the word art covers a wide range of disciplines, including painting, music, calligraphy, sculpture, dance, theater, opera, fashion, literature, and naturally, interior design. Other forms of art, notably painting, calligraphy, carving, and literature profoundly influence traditional Chinese interior design as an art form. It draws sustenance from a variety of art disciplines as it swims in the ocean of art.

In its use of colors and color coordination, traditional Chinese interior design is inspired by principles and techniques of traditional Chinese painting, and seeks to give literati touches to the interior space by using soft color tones and harmonious color combinations. In space arrangement, it adopts ideas and techniques similar to those of calligraphy. Chinese calligraphy is very particular about *bu bai* (the organization of blank and written spaces) and *jian jia* (the structure of a written character). Likewise, interior designers seek to achieve beauty in balance, both in the constituent parts and in the décor as a whole. In dealing with the shape of decorative objects traditional interior design is influenced by the art of carving and prizes the aesthetics of refinement and streamlined forms. In the creation of ambiance and aura Chinese interior design borrows from traditional literature the use of horizontal inscribed tablets and vertical couplets to give the space a theme and a desired feel.

Traditional Chinese interior design in its own way interprets and reflects the spirit and essence of these other art forms. It showcases the unique features of traditional Chinese painting by its use of the techniques of "giving equal attention to blank and painted spaces" and "purposefully leaving blank spaces." It creates aesthetic effects comparable to those of Chinese calligraphy with its harmonious organization of spaces and stable structures. Its ornate and refined decoration reflects the exquisite artistic skill sought by master carvers. In its creation of traditional interior and exterior spaces it gives concrete form to the idyllic scenarios celebrated in literature.

Nourished by the cultural heritage of a five-thousand-year-old civilization, Chinese traditional art possesses a large treasure trove of fine techniques and skills, and it sets as its goal the production of works with a rich cultural content. *Xie yi* (the writing of ideas, expression of the artist's sentiments with economical use of ink and brush) and *chuan shen* (conveying or bringing out the spirit, lifelike representation) are goals and characteristics shared by all traditional Chinese art forms. Influenced by other art forms, traditional Chinese interior design's ultimate goal is the creation of living spaces with a cultural imprint by using every possible means of design and decoration.

On facing page The white wall, the natural wood, and ocher-colored objects create a clean and harmonious color effect. The unsubstantial silhouette of the few plum twigs in the vase epitomizes the simple elegance of the space.

How Painting Colors Chinese Interior Spaces

The importance of colors to how an interior space looks and feels is obvious. The right colors are often an eye-catcher in the design and may set the tone for the interior. Since different colors affect people's feeling, state of mind, mood, and temperament in different ways, the designer must factor in the function of the room in question and the temperament of the person for whom the space is designed when choosing colors. Traditional Chinese interior design also has its own way of

The color scheme in this space exhibits a contrast between the warm wood color and the cooler gray green; on the other hand the two main color tones are both very bright. This mild contrast creates an ambience that has both vibrancy and quiet grace.

using colors, such as for the purpose of matching the Chinese style of decorating and construction. Sometimes using certain colors to paint the space will suffice to create a traditional Chinese look and feel.

Color use in traditional Chinese interior design has been deeply influenced by traditional Chinese painting, which uses the painting brush, ink, and pigments to create paintings on specially made rice paper (*xuan* paper) or silk. The genres of Chinese painting include literati painting, religious painting, Zen painting, Imperial court-style painting, folk painting, fan painting, landscape painting, light purple landscape painting, blue-green landscape painting, the minute and laborious technique of boneless (*mo gu*) style painting, ruled-line ink painting, thematic painting, *xie yi* painting, finger painting, miniature painting, ink painting, ink-and-color painting, white drawing, paintings featuring court ladies, animals, and still life. The colors used are generally quiet and muted except in folk paintings, which tend to have loud and flashy colors. There is rarely sharp contrast in the mix of colors. This kind of color palettes and principles of color matching are also seen in traditional Chinese interior design.

Distinctive Ways of Using Colors   Learned scholars appreciate and favor interiors whose color schemes follow the tradition of literati painting and court-style painting, characterized by light quiet colors, while the use of bright colors and strong contrast, as in folk paintings, is found more in interior designs with an ethnic or local flavor.

The light style is more popular in traditional interior design. as in the example of a signature Chinese décor consisting of white walls with wood furniture and ornaments. *Liu bai*, or the intentional leaving of blank spaces in art works, is an important technique in Chinese painting. It is required by the pictorial arrangement of the painting for the purpose of "ventilation." The positioning and proportions of these blanks directly affect the artistic effect and taste of the painting. In Chinese painting the artist expresses ideas "beyond the brush stroke" by using *liu bai*, which is a more subtle means of artistic expression than the brush, and can create artistic "landscapes of the mind" inaccessible to the brush. The white walls in traditional interior design play a role akin to the first function of *liu bai*—it acts like the painting paper, against which the wood furniture and ornaments are like the flowing strokes of the

In this photo, the contrast between the yellowish green cushions and the warmer color tone of the lamp and the painting coincides with the contrast between analogous colors employed in Chinese traditional painting. It enlivens the space without upsetting the overall understated tone.

This interior creates a typically Chinese look and feel by the use of clean, harmonious colors. The pair of narrow vertical paintings and a sprig of green vine on the wall express, in a *xie yi*, minimalist way recalling Chinese traditional painting, an aspiration to transcend the material world and achieve the union of man and nature.

brush. The light color acts also as counterweight to the more somber colors of wood, producing a greater visual appeal. In addition to this achromatic color, the use of cream color, beige, off-white, light green, and light brown is also common in the light style. The use of these colors taken from nature gives the interior a refreshing, novel quality and reflects the influence of ancient concepts of "emulating nature" and "transcending the quotidian world" in interior design.

Red is a color that probably best represents the Chinese. They consider it as a symbol of good luck and happiness, and its popularity in traditional interior design has never waned. It is used for something as expansive as a wall and as small as an ornamental object. Adding an accent of red instantly gives the interior a Chinese feel. The glittering gold undertone symbolizes wealth and prominence. The elegant and luxurious purple undertone implies good luck. All these are popular auspicious colors. Note that these stronger colors are mostly used on ornamental objects or trims and not directly on furniture or larger decorative items, with the exception of red painted wooden ornaments. This is another indication of the restraint inherent in the Chinese temperament.

Criteria of Color Matching   Traditional Chinese interior design prefers harmony over contrast in the matching of colors. The use of assorted colors is more for the purpose of adding accent than for an intentional clash of colors on large areas. As in the use of colors, color matching in a light-style décor leans toward the use of harmonious colors; contrasting colors are used only in small localized areas. In a brightly colored décor large-area contrasting colors may be used to create a decorative effect of color contrast.

As an aesthetic criterion, harmony is the state attained by two similar elements capable of creating a common order. The unity of the elements is essential to harmony: thus, the matching of color phases, tones, and brightness is capable of producing the effect of harmony. A harmonious matching of colors produces a soft and elegant effect—a "Confucian elegance."

Contrast is an aesthetic principle that calls for the matching of color elements widely different in color phase, tone, or brightness to achieve a strong stimulation. The color contrast used in traditional Chinese interior design is a light-dark contrast of achromatic colors, as in Chinese ink paintings. An example is the contrast between large areas of white walls and wooden ornaments that are unpainted or japanned. Contrast in color phases is seen in localized accents—"a spot of red in a mass of green," mainly to enliven the atmosphere by the use of small-area contrast. The more flashy use of the contrast of loud colors is

more often found in soft furnishings that are meant to exhibit a strong folksy flavor, such as handicraft articles, light fixtures, and fabrics. A retro Chinese-style design movement that is gaining popularity uses bright and lavish colors to create a decorative effect of strong contrast, possibly building on and exaggerating this color contrast used in soft furnishings. This is another aspect of the Chinese design scene.

Traditional Chinese interior design generally prefers soft and warm colors. This reflects the influence of traditional Chinese painting and is, to a large degree, attributable to the friendly, kind, and meek nature of the Chinese people.

The color use in this interior appears to adhere to a scheme of simplicity and purity—the wood furniture, whitewashed wall, even the painting, the cups and saucers, the vase and spray of flowers in it all tacitly acquiescing to this quiet color scheme. The tablecloth with rose-colored stripes adds a bright motif to the space without violating the harmony and unity of the color tone, and validates the understatement of the rest of the décor.

How Calligraphy Structures Chinese Interior Spaces

If colors, furnishings, and materials are the cosmetics and ornaments for an interior space, then the structure of the space is its frame or body. A successful interior design starts with a good structure, which sets the tone for the interior.

In a number of ways, traditional Chinese interior design is similar to traditional Chinese calligraphy in its management of the structure and layout of the interior spaces. Calligraphy is essentially a composed aesthetics in that it is very

With the pair of cups as anchor, the solid-looking loop-handled basket set on a delicate stand, will not feel top-heavy. Can you see an analogy between this arrangement and the care taken by a calligrapher to ensure good structural composition, both in individual characters and in the calligraphy work as a whole?

particular about the arrangement of the individual characters and of the work as a whole. It seeks an overall visual beauty and harmony. Likewise, there should be rhythm in space arrangement, alternating between airy and dense parts. The placement of furniture and the positioning of objects with the main color theme are like the brushstrokes in a calligraphic work. We will now compare Chinese calligraphy and traditional Chinese interior design from the viewpoint of robust lines, harmonious composition, and balanced structure—all criteria of good calligraphy.

Robust Lines   Lines are the most basic element in Chinese calligraphy; they are infinitely variable. For example, the brush can be lifted or pressed down in various directions. Ink and water content interact with a line in different ways. By shifting, the relationship and contrast between lines can be manipulated, changing the look of a character.

These richly varied lines are the building blocks of Chinese calligraphy. In interior spaces, these same building-block "lines" are present—in two-dimensional traditional design they may take the form of a set of symmetrically placed pieces of furniture; in three dimensions it may be a composition using converging lines to focus the viewer's eyes on a central hall, or a main color theme made up of several compatible colors, or perhaps the repeated appearance of some Chinese traditional ornamental symbol. They form visible and invisible lines in space and constitute a major component of interior design that contributes to the creation of the central theme of the space being designed. Note that they do not exist in isolation. Like the lines in calligraphy that have to interweave to form characters and columns of writing and then the complete work, these "lines" in an interior space have to interact at different levels and in different ways to produce the intended decorative

The lighted strips on the wall in the background create spatial depth and divide the surface into four parts, like so many strokes that compose a written Han character, producing dynamic movement without upsetting the overall coherence.

effect and produce an elegant style.

The "lines" in traditional Chinese interior
design usually follow set rules and constitute a
coherent whole, as in the regular script of Chinese
calligraphy. Of course, there are some design styles
influenced by Taoist and Buddhist thinking whose
"lines" run free and unfettered, as in the strokes of
the cursive script of Chinese calligraphy.

Harmonious Composition   Whether in a
symmetrical or "square" spatial arrangement or
a free, unorthodox layout, the quest for beauty is
both a goal and a principle in interior design, just
as a calligrapher desires harmony, suppleness,
grace and a free spirit in the overall composition
and the structure of the individual characters. An
important attribute of beauty is "harmony," which
is a principle of aesthetics and a law of nature. In
calligraphy excessive squatness or narrowness,
sparseness, excess fat, and lack of spine are
examples of disharmony. Mismanagement of space
in interior design is manifested in disproportion,
clutter, and excessive fragmentation or uniformity.
Harmony in interior space arrangement is achieved
by the selection of a suitable number of furniture
pieces of proper dimensions determined on the

basis of the function and size of the room being
designed. In addition to the proper arrangement of
the space being designed, attention should also be
paid to balance between the related spaces so as
to create a harmony of the whole and to realize the
desired tone and style.

Structural Balance   Stability and balance
are basic requirements of Chinese calligraphy.
The square Chinese characters were created with
reference to the beings and things in the world,
and it is only natural that they should reflect
the characteristics of stability and balance found
in them. Stability and balance are considered
attributes of beauty in traditional Chinese interior
design. Symmetry is a special form of the beauty
of balance and one of the most commonly applied
principles in traditional Chinese interior design.
Symmetry evokes orthodoxy and stability. In
addition to absolute symmetry, the beauty of
balance often takes other, more exuberant forms
in interior design, such as recurrent pattern,
contrast, and the juxtaposition of the primary
and the secondary. For example, in traditional
Chinese interior design, the furniture combination
of a table and two chairs is often placed not only

The black roof tiles in this corner of a Chinese garden can be likened to brushstrokes flowing across the whitewashed wall, spinning yarns about the millennial Chinese culture.

On facing page The horizontal lines of the treads and the vertical lines of the balustrade, the solidity of the landing between the two flights, and the slenderness of the wooden newel posts create, with contrast and balance, a harmonious space.

in symmetry along the central axis in the central hall of the principal building to set the tone for the house, but also in other parts of the central hall and in other rooms, such as the study. This recurrent theme produces a sense of structural balance in a space or between several spaces. As mentioned previously, the enclosed courtyard, an inward-looking exterior space in traditional Chinese architecture, is a special part of the interior space. As a "non-present" space in natural light framed in a "present" space in shade, the courtyard and the room form a structural balance based on this contrast.

Space arrangement ideas in traditional Chinese interior design, such as the hierarchy of rooms and the configuration consisting of one public and two private rooms, are already fully vetted in the stage of architectural planning. These ideas serve as a basis for interior space planning. Traditional Chinese interior design takes these space planning ideas and applies them to the details of space arrangement and design. Just as in traditional Chinese calligraphy, attention is equally paid to the beauty in the arrangement of individual strokes of each character and the beauty in the composition as a whole, traditional Chinese interior design also seeks beauty and harmony of the parts and the whole that ultimately result in an interior space with a sense of depth.

How Carving Molds Chinese Interior Spaces

Diao liang hua dong (ornately carved beams and painted rafters) is an oft-cited expression in describing traditional Chinese architecture and interiors. The use of elaborate carving and fine painting as a decorative means is typical of traditional Chinese interior design. Ornate is indeed the general impression people have of traditional Chinese décors. Fine carvings are ubiquitous in traditional Chinese architecture and interiors: carved structural elements such as columns, crossbeams, and column brackets; decorative elements such as openwork windows, partition boards, and floor screens; decorative animal figures on roofs, eaves-tile ornaments, caisson

The finely carved scenery, buildings, boats, and flowers on this structural element showcase the fine craftsmanship typically seen in traditional Chinese wood carving.

A decorative object commonly found outside traditional buildings in China, this stone lion carved in the round, with its head innocently turned to one side and a paw placed on an embroidered ball, is a symbol of good luck.

ceilings; carved stone ramps, thresholds, floral floor tiles; big items such as decorative archways that are sculptures in their own right; details such as open, hand-carved trims featured on furniture and carved base plates for flower vases.

Carving is one of the earliest plastic arts in China to come into widespread use. It can be said that it is the mother of handicraft. In antiquity,

people carved fine images on rough stone columns to represent the gods they worshipped. That's how carving started. In the beginning, carvings were decorative and aspired to emulate nature before they developed into human figures with facial expressions and body postures. Then they took on the functions of praising exploits and virtues, passing folklore on to future generations and

commemoration until, after centuries of evolution, it has developed into an art capable of creating lively artistic images on inert natural objects. There are many genres of carving. Depending on the material used, those commonly found in architecture and interior spaces are stone, brick, wood, bamboo, jade, and porcelain.

Stone Carving   Due to its hardness and resistance against erosion, stone is widely used in structural members, including door frames, railings, embracing drum, ramps, plinths, and crossbeams; adjunct stone structures, including monuments, lions, ornamental columns, and statues; and indoor decorative stone display items, including incense burners and the "Five Sacrificial Utensils." The contrast between fine craftsmanship and rough material in stone carvings produces a solid decorative effect of lasting appeal.

Brick Carving   The traditional art of brick carving evolved from the making of eave tile ends in the Eastern Zhou dynasty (770 – 256 BC) and the pictorial bricks in the Han dynasty. The

quality requirements are stricter for gray bricks in the selection of raw material, and in the molding and firing processes. As a result, the gray bricks are harder and have a finer surface suitable for carving. Landscapes, flowers, and human figures carved on gray bricks constitute an important art form in ancient Chinese architectural carving. They are used mainly to decorate structural members and wall surfaces in temples and civilian dwellings. In terms of practical functions and aesthetic values, brick carvings used by common folks tend to be simple and down-to-earth in appearance and style; for them, refinement and elaborateness are less important than sturdiness of the structural members and their weather resistance. In upscale residences for the rich and powerful and in imperial palaces, the brick carvings have to meet the highest standards of craftsmanship and no effort is spared to create an ornate opulence, sometimes by the addition of clay sculptures or porcelain inlays. In the late Qing dynasty (1644 – 1911) especially, brick carving became so elaborate and refined that it took on the allure of artistic painting.

This wooden bracket shows a beautiful, streamlined pattern of auspicious clouds in bas relief, accented by vivid relief carvings of flowers and plants.

On facing page *Diao liang hua dong* (ornately carved beams and painted rafters) is an apt description of this space whose structural elements are all richly decorated with fine carvings.

Carving is not only a decorative technique in traditional Chinese interior design, but also represents an aesthetic preference for elaborateness and ornateness. In this design, a rich decorative effect is achieved through the contrast between the finely carved panels and the rough texture of the stone statues.

Wood Carving Wood structures are one of the most common forms of construction in traditional Chinese architecture, and timber is the most popular material used in interior construction and decoration. For this reason, decorative carvings found in traditional Chinese building exteriors and interiors are predominantly wood, which fall under one of the three categories of carving—round, root, and relief. As building decoration, carving in the round is often seen in Buddha statues and other decorative artifacts. Root carving covers handicrafts, small stationery items, and furniture such as "natural" tables (crafted around natural objects). Common examples of relief and half relief carving are found on architectural structural members. Hollow carvings are also found on partition boards with a rosette pattern and floor screens. There are also many instances where these different carving techniques are used in combination for interior decoration. Wood carving is used very often on structural members. Trees whose tough timber is of a fine, dense texture, such as found in cypress, sandalwood, camphor wood, cedar, and rosewood, are selected for this purpose because of their warp resistant quality. In wood carving the artist will have plenty of subjects

or styles to choose from and will find the material eminently suitable for the expression of artistic themes.

Other Genres of Carving Bamboo carving, jade carving, and porcelain carving are commonly found in furniture, stationery, and ornamental objects. Literati prize bamboo for its symbolism of high-minded purity and therefore carved bamboo objects, such as sculpted bamboo brush pots and carved bamboo vertical couplets have a large presence in the scholar's study. They suit the scholarly ambiance of the study. The elegant and noble jade has always been thought of as a symbol of good quality and Confucian virtue. Jade was used in some of the earliest Chinese carvings, but the use of this rare material in architectural decoration is limited to ornamental objects such as flower vases and carved river jade displays (with carving in only one part of a stone) or carved jade pieces in the form of inlays in furniture or structural members. Porcelain carving combines painting and carving. It uses a special technique that carves works of painting and calligraphy on uncolored white porcelain. Carved utensils like plates, bowls, vases, tea things, and stationery are functional; but carvings on porcelain plates

The door panel of this bedside cabinet displays both diversity and depth in the decorative effect created by the line carving, low relief carving, and openwork carving techniques employed in its detailing.

placed on rosewood display stands are artworks. The technique of hollow carving is also used in porcelain carvings. An example is the auspicious patterns and symbols hollow-carved into porcelain drum stools.

The traditional Chinese art of carving not only supplies fine works of art for the decoration of interior spaces, but has also influenced the aesthetics of form in traditional interior design. This can be seen in the design of traditional Chinese furniture, such as master armchairs, tables with the scroll terminations, altar consoles, and washbasin stands, which exhibit flowing lines and elegant forms that serve both practical and decorative purposes.

How Literature Sets the Tone of Chinese Interior Spaces

The decoration of a building and its interior spaces with literary art works is probably a unique feature of traditional Chinese interior design. These art works include horizontal inscribed tablet (*bian-e*) , vertical inscribed couplets (*ying lian)*, large painting or calligraphy scroll hung in the central hall (*zhong tang*), single narrow hanging scroll (*tiao ping),* and other kinds of calligraphic works. These works blend perfectly into the building environment in content, form, material, and style. They add interest and life to the environment and, in return, being showcased by it. The intellectual and literary tenor of these art works adds a cultural flair to the interior, making them an indispensable part of traditional Chinese buildings.

In the millennia since its inception Chinese literature has forged a distinctive identity with its unique content, forms, styles, aesthetic ideals, a vibrant intellectual and cultural heritage, and a system of theoretical criticism. Chinese literature is a jewel of the crown of world literature given its long history, diverse forms, numerous authors, voluminous works, unique styles, distinctive character, and charm. The inscribed tablets and couplets decorating Chinese buildings, like the diverse kinds of poetic works, are a form of traditional Chinese literature. But unlike those literary works, which are bound into books and collections, they go into buildings and rooms to become part of them and express in distilled language the aspirations, culture, refined taste, and interests of the person who chooses the décor, and boldly and lyrically enunciate the theme and spirit of the interior design. These works of art can be said to be the definition, theme and soul of the interior space they decorate.

Horizontal Inscribed Tablet   A horizontal inscribed tablet hung above a door serves as decoration, reflects the name and nature of the building, and enunciates moral doctrine or expresses a sentiment in a literary and artistic

These stylized Chinese characters not only help clarify the essence of the design but also provide an excellent decorative element.

You may not find a single written character in this space, but the chair waiting for a guest under the red plum blossoms, the empty birdcage, and the variegated brick wall pique the viewer's interest like an unfinished story, or a poem with a subtle meaning.

form. Strictly speaking, *bian* enunciates moral values and express sentiments and *e* describes the name and nature of the building. *Bian e* are normally hung above doors or under eaves. When a building has doors on all four sides, a *bian* may be hung above any of those doors, but it is mandatory above the front door. Horizontal inscribed tablet encapsulate the best of verse and

other literary writing circulating in the ocean of Chinese culture, and the skills of calligraphy, seal cutting, carving, and coloring go into their making. Using succinct verse, fine calligraphy, and thought-provoking metaphors, they comment on current affairs and important personalities. They are indeed fine specimens of Chinese culture. Horizontal inscribed tablet can be grouped by function into

This rockery is covered with the character 醉 (*zui*, intoxicated) carved into the stone in a variety of styles. Looking at the scene may be enough to intoxicate you.

On facing page Vertical couplets and horizontal inscribed tablet can define the function of the space and capture its essence.

categories such as clan name tablet (*tang hao bian*), tablet on commemorative arches (*pai fang bian*), celebratory and festive tablet (*xi qing bian*), shop name tablet (*zi hao bian*), and tablet inscribed with calligraphy of invited notables (*ti zi bian*). Grouped by material used for the tablets, they roughly fall under the categories of stone, wood, and adobe-type horizontal inscribed tablet. A horizontal inscribed tablet is the humble "dotted i (eye)" that makes a traditional Chinese building come alive. Whether the horizontal inscribed tablet offers a description of the physical environment and landscape, or extols the virtues of the clan, is an expression of good wishes or reflects the aspirations of the person who commissioned it, the viewer will gain a deeper insight into the intent and spirit of the design, and the tone of the designed space will come into sharper focus.

Vertical Inscribed Couplets   Originally a subcategory of vertical couplets, vertical inscribed couplets has with time become another name for vertical couplets. A *ying* is one of the two front columns in a traditional Chinese hall. In early days vertical inscribed couplets were normally hung on these front columns. The verse form of the vertical inscribed couplets was a great innovation

in traditional Chinese literary arts. It evolved from an ornate rhythmical prose (*pian ti wen*) of the Han dynasty (206 BC – 220 AD) and Wei Kingdom period (220 – 265) and the regulated poetry of the Tang dynasty (618 – 907). Characterized by an ornate style, parallelism, rhythmical arrangement, and musicality, it is combined with the best of the two worlds of powerful prose and rhythmical Verse to convey deep meaning and metaphor with a frugality of language, these couplets on scrolls have remained popular among the Chinese. vertical inscribed couplets and horizontal inscribed tablet are normally seen together and are referred to as *bian lian*. Textually, the horizontal inscribed tablet usually sums up what is said in the vertical inscribed couplets and is sometimes referred to as a horizontal inscription (*heng pi*). The vertical inscribed couplets can often be an extension of and elaboration on the horizontal inscribed tablet. The horizontal inscribed tablet and the two couplets form a visually stable pictorial composition of one horizontal stroke supported on two vertical ones, producing a decorative effect of balance and symmetry.

Calligraphic Works   Calligraphic works such as *zhong tang* (large painting or calligraphy work

The ambience of an interior doesn't have to be abstract. When one passes through this corridor of inscribed tablets, the functionality, and personality of the space unfold like pages of a book.

hung in the central hall), *tiao ping* (single narrow hanging scroll), and *tang ping* (set of four narrow scrolls hung side by side) are also used for interior decoration. They highlight the talents, breadth of vision, learning, and aspirations of the person for whom the interior space is designed. A large work of painting or calligraphy is hung in the middle of the central hall of a traditional Chinese residence. It is usually a rectangular scroll (length greater than width) with the calligraphy running vertically. The central hall is the most important space in a traditional Chinese house and it goes without saying the importance of the *zhong tang* scroll in

decorative and intellectual terms. Hanging scrolls are another form used in the mounting and framing of Chinese paintings and calligraphies. Those hung singly are called *tiao ping*, and sets of four scrolls hung side by side are called *tang ping*. In traditional Chinese buildings the *zhong tang* scroll is hung beneath the horizontal inscribed tablet of the central hall (*tang bian*) and flanked on the east and west by four *tiao ping* scrolls. Vertical inscribed couplets hung on the columns in the hall represent another indispensable decorative element and technique.

An apt description of the importance of literary

art works such as horizontal inscribed tablet and vertical inscribed couplets in architecture and interior design is found in the following remark in the Chinese literary classic *A Dream of Red Mansions*: "Without the embellishment of calligraphy this vast landscaped garden with its gazebos and pavilions will be dull and boring. It will lose its luster despite the flowers, the willow trees and mounds, and ponds." Traditional Chinese literature in the form of calligraphic art works decorates architectural spaces; the literary moods created in Chinese literature and its refined aesthetic taste also influence the choices of ambiance and tastes in interior design. In many traditional Chinese architectural environments one can find evidence of the influence of some beautiful natural scenery or an inspiring scene drawn from some literary masterpiece. Since interior design is a relatively implicit way of expressing thoughts, a first impression of the beauty of a décor needs to be supplemented by a careful reading of the inscriptions on the horizontal inscribed tablet and vertical inscribed couplets that encapsulate the spirit of the décor in order for the viewer to fully appreciate the intent and ingenuity of the design.

Chapter 3

Local Customs
in Chinese Interior Design

Chinese characters are extremely interesting. Take the example of the character 俗 (custom) in the chapter's title. It is composed of two parts, "people" on the left and "grain" on the right. It could be taken to mean that common folks need to sustain themselves on grains, as opposed to immortals that don't. It could also be understood as what is commonly recognized or accepted by people who cultivate grains, that is, what is most popular and most commonly seen, as in 俗称 (*su cheng* or commonly known as), 俗名 (*su ming* or commonly called). Or, the part denoting "grain" can also be understood as a microcosm of nature, and the combination of people and grain would denote people in a natural environment, and also the customs and conventions formed by people after living and working in that environment for a long time.

What we call "customary" is exactly the result of a long-term mutual influence between people and nature and their interactions. It includes limits imposed by nature on people and the material civilization they created by accepting and transforming nature on one hand, and the spiritual civilization they formed after living and working in that natural environment for a long time on the other. Through analyzing the traditional Chinese style interior design we can see very clearly how hard people have worked and the achievements they have accomplished in those two areas, as reflected in design styles of different local and cultural flavors.

You may say that China before the industrial revolution was an agricultural country with vast expanses, a sparse population, and rich natural resources, and its architecture and interior design were limited by the location and the local materials available; but it is more accurate to say that the importance attached to the ancient concept of ensuring "synergy among climate, location, and people" is the major and deeper reason behind the Chinese emphasis of harmonious coexistence of people and nature in mutual development. The use of natural resources found locally to build and decorate architectural spaces and the creation of a setting and style that is in harmony with the natural environment will not only facilitate and ease the construction work, it will also ensure that the living space is a natural extension of the outside environment. Such an architectural design would be safe, durable, and less costly, and can also satisfy the all-round physical and psychological needs of the people.

The traditional way of adapting interior design to localities and the availability of local material largely reflects the integration with the physical elements of the natural environment. In fact, interior design also has a spiritual side that reflects the myriads of regional and local customs and culture. A careful observation of the specific design layout and unique furnishing of different types of traditional interior design, can offer us a glimpse of the brilliant assortment of local customs and culture of China that govern the daily lives of people, their food, clothing, shelter, and transportation as well as their arts.

This is exactly what traditional Chinese interior design is about. From a perspective closest to real life and through an art form, it reflects and tells us about the environment, the living conditions as well as the associated civilization and culture, it is nothing less than an epic history that carries no sounds and no words. Yet it is so vivid and vibrant.

On facing page The blue floral porcelain vase and the wooden box with floral carvings are not so much articles of handicraft as they are utensils of everyday use. Even the gardenia in the vase exudes a familiar fragrance that is reminiscent of Grandma's home.

Adaptation to the Natural Environment

Interior design as an art close to life needs to be both artistic and functional, that is, to have a beautiful and eye-pleasing outlook and to offer convenience and comfort. In the final analysis, the design is meant to create a safe, durable, comfortable, and beautiful internal environment. If we are to say that the livability of a space depends on its safety and durability, then the quality of life inside the space will depend on its comfort and beauty. And the element of "comfort," defined as a response to use requirements necessitated by objective needs, is considered very critical. Even with the same living space, a different external natural environment may give rise to diametrically different interior requirements. It is in the process of satisfying these different requirements that

different esthetic tendencies and styles with distinctive local characteristics come into being.

The styles of interior design are displayed mainly in the layout, color, model, and furnishing details. And the impact of the natural environment, including geographical, climate, and resource conditions, on traditional Chinese interior design can also be observed in the following areas.

Space Layout   Climate conditions are undoubtedly the most direct and influential element when it comes to the external natural environment that affects space layout. Dramatically different climate conditions in different provinces, municipalities, and regions are to be expected in the large expanse of the Chinese territory. In

In the bitterly cold winters in north China, most daily activities are carried out on a raised platform heated from below. This way of life shaped by the need to adapt to the natural environment has led to a unique form of space arrangement.

This sky well (*tian jing*), an interior court or atrium typical of traditional dwellings in Huizhou (southern Part of Anhui Province and Wuyuan County, Jiangxi Province today) fulfills multiple functions, such as ventilation, natural lighting, water drainage, etc. In light of local climate conditions the space is kept narrow and enclosed within high walls to prevent over-exposure to sunlight.

general, the interior space layout in the temperate and hot zones in the south tends to be loose and flexible, and more attention is given to air circulation and avoiding over-exposure to the sun; whereas the space layout in the colder regions to the north tends to be more concentrated and closely-set, and more attention is given to having more sun exposure and better heat retention. For instance, in traditional residences in the south, beds and desks are often arranged right next to the window. The furniture pieces are less imposing so to ease air circulation and take full advantage of daylight. But in the north, large spaces are often subdivided into smaller ones to form better-insulated warm chambers and screened partitions. Some even arrange the layout around the center

Charcoal, a venting hood, and the rows of trunks in this room conjure images of a nomadic life.

of a raised platform heated from below, a brazier, or other heating devices. Secondly, space layout is also related to geographical conditions. A case in point is the sprawling multi-courtyard house with ample building space on flat terrain and the terraced design of buildings expanded in a vertical direction in mountainous areas because of topographical limitations. These differences in space layout are inseparable from the physical and psychological impact of the natural environment on people. Another factor in space layout is the level of development: living spaces in more developed regions are relatively small because of higher population density, so for them, a flexible and compact layout is more suitable. But less developed and sparsely populated regions can certainly afford a more liberal space layout.

Color Arrangement   A smart color arrangement in interior design can add beauty to the space, is also a reflection of the personality of the master, and in turn can affect the mood and emotions of the people living there. As differentiated by region, in the north, warm colors are preferred to dispel the melancholy brought on by the cold weather. In the south, cool and lighter tones, or a combination without color, are often used to lessen the effect of the heat. On the other hand, in more civilized urban areas, the choice of interior colors tends to be muted and reserved. The color combination stresses overall harmony with localized contrast. However, villages in the border areas tend to use bolder colors and strong contrasts to reflect the unpretentious and uninhibited nature of the local customs and people.

Furnishing Styles   In general, traditional interior furnishings tend to be more delicate and refined in the south and bold and expansive in the north. In the final analysis, this is a reflection of the differences in personality and tastes shaped by the natural environment. Southern China, notably the lower reaches of the Yangtze valley, is known for its beautiful landscape, rich resources, and high levels of education. Its interior design is characterized by elegance and fine taste that is marked by the delicate and intricate furnishings. This is not only the result of an aesthetic choice, it is also a response to the natural environment. A case in point is the chicken cage cupboard that is quite popular in the south. The cupboard is surrounded on three sides by open lattice, looks cute, and allows air to circulate freely. The design ensures that food can stay unspoiled longer in the hot and humid conditions of the south. Another example is the "legged" furniture that has become a feature of southern-style furniture. With its graceful lines and intricate carvings, the "legs" are meant to keep the furniture piece from direct contact with the ground. In the expansive north, which is characterized by a sweeping and magnificent landscape with a long history and cultural tradition, the interior design style tends to be more prudent and solemn. Its furnishings tend to be square-shaped, symmetrical, and bigger in size. For coastal regions or port cities that are more open to the outside world, the furnishing styles tend to be more fashion-oriented with a touch of foreign influence. Their interior counterparts are more conservative and traditional in comparison.

Decorative Elements   The same north-south differences are seen in the decorative elements of furnishing styles. Taking advantage of its mild climate, south China often favors flower arrangements, bonsais, and other natural landscapes for decoration, whereas the north prefers tapestry, rock landscaping, flower vases, and other decorative objects. As for the materials used for decorating, wooden carving, bamboo crafts, and straw plaiting are often found in traditional interior design in the south. Brick carvings and stone carvings are often seen in the north. When using the same carving technique for interior decoration, hollowed-out carvings are more common in the south and more solid relief or semi-relief carvings are common in the north. The differences reflect different esthetic preferences in the north and south, and their respective adaptation to the natural environment.

Aside from the above-mentioned aspects, adaptation to nature has also found expression in the architectural design, landscape design, and material use of traditional Chinese architecture. Of course, Chinese architecture has no monopoly on this feature and wisdom. It is a universal phenomenon. Indeed, its application should not be limited to traditional architecture. Its design concept, very much in step with the modern concept of environmental protection, needs to be preserved and further developed.

In humid, rain-rich southeast China, buildings often feature openwork windows and doors, gauze curtains, and bamboo curtains as a means to improve air circulation and natural lighting. The use of bamboo basketry with a distinct local color as decoration is an example of adaptation to the natural environment.

Use of Local Materials

The use of materials that are produced in abundance and commonly seen in the local area for construction and interior furnishing is not only convenient, but also a reflection of the wisdom of conforming to nature. Because of different geographies and climates, every location or region has its specific micro-environment. The plants grown here, the minerals produced here, and the people who lived here have no doubt come to terms with the environment after a long period of coexistence and adaptation. The use of local materials to build and furnish their living spaces is not only convenient and practical, but also ensures safety and durability. Moreover, you are what you eat and what you breathe. In time, your body will adapt to and be at equilibrium with the local environment, and your emotions and temperament will take on the local color. The use of local materials for interior design can then produce a style that appeals to local esthetics and tastes.

The vast Chinese territory includes regions with dissimilar geological conditions and species of vegetation. In traditional interior design, distinct regional styles are formed when people build and furnish with locally available materials, such as stone, bricks, wood, bamboo, rattan, straw, and fabrics that meet the requirements for strength and durability.

Stone   Any building space constructed with stone and furnished with stone carvings can immediately convey a sense of rugged solidness through the rough texture and traces of the chisel. It is as if the owner of the house, a towering figure with a low voice, is trying to take us on an emotional journey through the harness of his life. This seems to be the typical image and personality of the people in the north and in the mountainous areas of China. In contrast to the smooth and sophisticated people of the south, they are known to be straightforward and generous in nature, with characteristics as steady and down-to-earth as the locally produced stone. In regions abundant with stone, its strength and durability make it a choice material for roads, bridges, and walls. The gorgeous colors and different textures of granite, marble, and blue stone are used to furnish the external and internal spaces of buildings. Stone

This suite of bamboo furniture attests to the wisdom of local sourcing. The use of bamboo matches local climate conditions and the resident's temperament and taste.

carvings and cuttings further enrich the decorative details through a variety of techniques such as light engraving, relief carving, hollow carving, and carving in the round.

Brick   Bricks are made of clay. Since clay is widely available in China, it has been used extensively in traditional building construction and furnishing. Its earliest use can be traced back to the Zhou dynasty (c.1046 – 256 BC) about two thousand years ago. In numerous traditional buildings, bricks were used for walls, flooring, and roof tiles, which were made of construction-grade clay. Bricks made locally are low cost and durable,

and have the qualities of being fire-proof, heat-retaining, sound-proof, and moisture-absorbent. That's why even until today bricks and their improved versions are still the most commonly used building material. Their decorative value for traditional buildings should not be overlooked either. Pressed designs on bricks, painted bricks, decorative eaves-tiles, and elaborate tile carvings have added exquisite details and beauty to traditional spaces and given them regional characters through rich and colorful techniques and styles.

Wood   Literally earth and wood, the last two

In localities with an abundance of stone, people take full advantage of the material's hardness, beautiful grain, and suitability for carving in construction and decorating.

This bamboo screen, with
its natural lines and unique
texture, is a bright spot in the
space. It is a testimony to the
benefit of using local materials
in design and decoration.

characters of the Chinese expression *da xing tu mu*,
or undertaking a big construction project, stand for
construction. The importance of earth and wood
for traditional architecture is self-evident. "Earth"
refers to the bricks and tiles mentioned above, and
"wood" refers to timber of various kinds used for
construction and furnishing. Traditional building
construction is composed of two parts: civil work
and furnishing work, which in building parlance
are known as *da mu zuo*, or framing carpentry and
xiao mu zuo, or finish carpentry. Framing work
used mostly timber for beams, columns, and roof
trusses. This kind of wood structure was the most
popular because it was strong and earthquake
resistant. For finish carpentry work, wood was
extensively used for inside and outside furnishing
and decoration, including for doors, windows,
railings, room partitions, caisson ceilings, furniture,
decorative moldings and objects, and even articles
for daily use. Wood as a material is long lasting
and particularly suitable for decorative purposes.
It is easy to work with and can either be carved
or chiseled. It is no exaggeration to say that
there would be no traditional Chinese architecture
without wood.

Bamboo, Rattan and Straw   The warm and

humid climate of south China supports a lush growth of a variety of plant species. Since ancient times Chinese people have learned to benefit from nature's endowments. They used bamboo, rattan, and plants from the rush family for building and interior decoration. Bamboo has the same durability as wood when used to build houses, pavilions, and bridges. Moreover, it has a unique natural beauty. Furniture pieces, partitions, and small ornaments and utensils made of bamboo were especially preferred by scholars and men of letters for their inherent natural elegance. Rattan and straw were often used in the seats of chairs and couches, their weaving pattern and texture offer a chic sensibility, and furthermore, they provide a soothing relief from the hot and humid weather.

Fabrics The role of fabrics in traditional interior design should never be underestimated. Common fabrics used were cotton, flax, and silk. Since they are all natural material, this serves as a further proof of the use of local materials for interior decoration. As stated before, the overall style of traditional Chinese architecture tends to stress dignity and elegance, but the occasional use of fabric decoration can add to the variety of materials and provide color embellishment. Hence, wool tapestry, silk drapery, and different types of seat and back cushion have all been familiar design elements for traditional spaces. Fabrics have also been an indispensable component in many traditional Chinese furnishings, with two examples such as drapery for the alcove bedstead *ba bu Chuang* and lace curtains for bookshelves. Therefore, it is clear that fabric, in addition to its decorative value, also has a practical value as a space partition, a wind shield, a heat retainer, and dust and insect repellent.

Low productivity in ancient times was one of the contributing factors to the use of local materials for construction and interior design. And yet, it is precisely because of it that the traditional Chinese architecture has left us with brilliant interior design achievements along with a history marked by numerous schools and different styles. What is more important is that the concept of "harmonious co-existence with nature," a concept that dates back to Chinese antiquity, needs to be given full recognition and be relearned today when productivity is high, and when we realize that the high-energy-consumption construction business will have to go green in the interest of sustainable development.

Wood and cotton paper are very common materials, but with ingenuity and thoughtfulness, novel and interesting designs can be created with them.

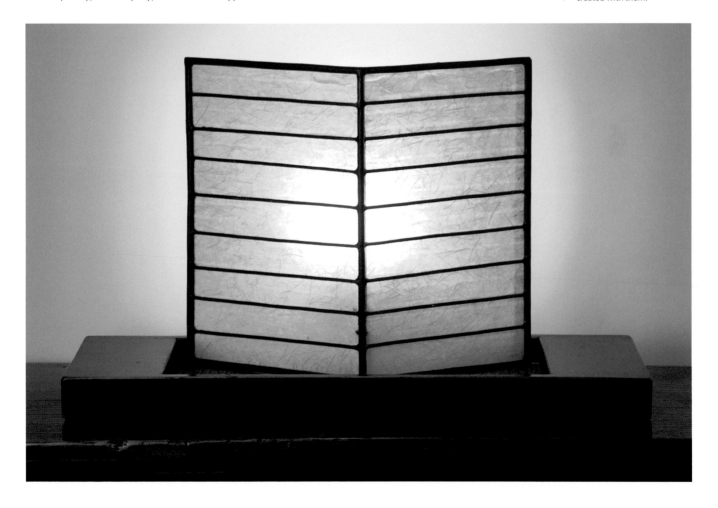

Expression of Folk Culture

China is a huge country, and as the Chinese saying goes, "customs change in as little as ten *li* (5 kilometers)," even people of the same ethnicity may have diametrically different customs and culture. Thus, Chinese folk culture is rich and colorful. Folklore refers to popular convention. It is the living culture created and shared by the general population of a country or nation and passed down from generation to generation. It is the part of culture that is closest to the body, mind, and life

The lacquered box and the paper cut with fine, intricate patterns reflect the aesthetic preference for loud colors is characteristic of folk art. Their bright red color adds to the festive mood created by the fabric wall art.

of the people. There are folklores about physical labor, daily lives, and traditional holidays. As such, they are also reflected in traditional Chinese interior design.

Folk culture is mostly expressed in design layout and furnishing. Unique space layout often reflects family customs, *feng shui*, and the wish for good fortune, whereas interior furnishing and display have more to do with festival celebration, food, costume and accessories, folk arts and crafts, and numerous other folk cultures.

Family Customs Traditional Chinese family customs govern hierarchy and etiquettes. The

Chinese have always attached great importance to the family and have the fine tradition of upholding filial piety and respect for the elderly. There are also other norms and etiquettes to be observed in daily life. These all found expression in the functional arrangements and allocation of space. Take, for example, the courtyard house, which is the typical dwelling of north China. The south-facing principal rooms are reserved for parents and members of the older generation, while the accommodations for children and members of the younger generation are in the east or west wing. The master and his family used the inner courts, while guest and servant quarters are arranged

The two articles of wood handicraft are traditional Chinese food utensils. The use of these objects of simple traditional form and color as ornaments in the dining room evokes the time-honored culinary culture of China.

On facing page The cloth tiger, the rattle drum, and the pair of hand-made straw sandals are typical examples of folk handicraft. They have the same simplicity of the pebbles in the picture.

along the outer court. Important rooms such as reception halls are part of the principal rooms along the central axis, and secondary rooms such as the toilet and the kitchen are mostly assigned to the wings or to rooms facing north. These established space layouts and arrangement are a reflection of the orthodox and prudent nature of the people in northern china.

Feng Shui Customs   Space layout can also tell us much about people's belief in *feng shui* and wish for good fortune. As we said before, the common Chinese people are very particular about the location of the living room, bedrooms, and kitchen since they believe that it holds the key to the health and fortune of members of the family. According to the beliefs of *feng shui*, mirrors, fish

tanks, and green plants placed in a certain position can court good fortune and avoid misfortune, a design technique to "keep the evil spirit away."
In addition, to have a niche for a Buddhist statue, to have a Buddha on display or to have articles, emblems, and symbols of religious significance in the interior; the placement of a vase (*hua ping*), mirror (*jing zi*), a clock (*zhong*) on the hall table believed to ensure *zhong shen ping jing*, or lifelong peace, with *zhong*, *ping* and *jing* sharing the same sound found in the Chinese words for clock, vase and mirror respectively, all speak of the popular wish for good luck and peace.

Holiday Celebration Customs   Celebrating the New Year and other holidays has been important for the Chinese since ancient times. As the holiday

There is an unmistakable southern Chinese charm and elegance in the outwardly plain and simple winnowing basket of osier and the napkin of hand-woven cloth. Ordinary Chinese derive great joys and pleasures from simple, unimpressive-looking things, such as the *zongzi* (dumplings made of glutinous rice wrapped in bamboo leaves) in the bamboo steamer and the handful of lotus seeds in the bowl made of crude clay.

arrives, some decoration for the occasion in the interior can add to the festivity and showcase the colorful customs of holiday celebration. For instance, during the Spring Festival, the most important traditional Chinese holiday, every household is expected to post couplets, hang New Year paintings or pictures, and put up paper cut window decorations. Some households would also hang pairs of red lanterns to pray for prosperity, good luck, and health. For the Dragon Boat Festival, people would hang flag leaves on doors and perfume sachets inside the house to repel evil spirits. In addition, kites for the Pure Brightness Festival, lanterns for the Lantern Festival and others can all serve as intricate festival craftwork for interior decoration.

Food Customs In China, articles related to food can also be used as decoration for their folkloric appeal. For instance, beautifully wrought dainty pieces such as food baskets, cake molds, and exquisite tea sets, once put on display on window sills or etageres would immediately add

The character 囍 (*xi*, double happiness) seen on the red cushion is an indispensable motif in traditional weddings. The motif of brightly colored peony blossoms on another cushion adds to the sense of prosperity and good fortune.

a classical touch to the room. On the other hand, ears of golden-colored corn, ruby red hot peppers, and lovely round heads of garlic dangling in front of the window would bring to the room an unpretentious and natural country flavor.

Folk Costumes and Accessories   The culture of ancient Chinese costumes has a long and unique history. Although many of the costumes of bygone dynasties are no longer suitable for everyday wear, they are still special art pieces for their chic styles and beautiful handwork, and can be used for interior decoration. Furthermore, highly decorated headwear, exquisite jewelry, and finely made textiles with graceful designs worn by different ethnic minorities have often been used in interior decoration to showcase the rich and colorful folk costumes of China.

Folk Art   As opposed to orthodox art, folk art tends to be more personal and free in style. For those who have a special fondness for folk art,

a space decorated with local opera costumes, shadow show props, national musical instruments or peasant paintings, paper-cut work, craftwork made of clay, kaolin, bamboo or rattan, or cloth dolls, figurines, and other articles, speaks not only of their own taste but also their ardent love for local customs and folk art.

There are numerous categories of customs in addition to the ones mentioned above. There are also production, etiquette, and science and technology customs. But their roles in traditional interior design are less obvious and direct. Moreover, China is a country of many ethnicities, each of which has its own set of unique and fascinating customs and culture. We can only devote the limited space in this book to a description and analysis of the traditional customs of the Han ethnicity, which is the largest group in China.

The tea set features lotus flowers, which symbolize a good life, and a mandarin, which represents a successful career. These auspicious motifs that reflect common folk's honest wishes form part of folk culture.

Chapter 4

Incorporation of Diverse Styles
into Chinese Interiors

In the field of interior design, "mix and match" is a technique used to combine decorative elements from different geographical regions, cultural backgrounds, and design styles. It uses an assortment of multiple means of decoration to create a whole new visual effect and sensation distinct from tradition. "Mix" denotes the design technique used, but the purpose and key of this technique lie in the word "match." In other words, diverse techniques and elements may be used but a harmonious and coherent theme is the ultimate objective.

"Mix and match" is now widely used in creating Chinese-style interior designs. In fact, as China's contact with foreign cultures has grown and deepened in the last hundreds of years, there are many examples of outside influence in many areas of Chinese design. Patterns of Western painting on clay and ceramic utensils and the baroque-style legs for the furniture pieces of the Qing dynasty come to mind. They represent the beginnings of the "mix and match" concept. Art Deco, "integration of the old and the new," and "combination of the indigenous and the foreign" are some of the more typical techniques of "mix and match."

Art Deco originated and flourished in the 1920s and 1930s in Europe and the U.S. and was the most dominated design style in all areas in Shanghai at the time. As a decorative and design style, it serves as a transition from classicalism to modernism, its inclusion of classical esthetic principles and its adaptability to industrial production have simplified the traditional decorative elements and retained the qualities of beauty and human touch, which in itself can be understood as an expression of the "mix and match" concept. As to the "integration of the old and new" and the "combination of the indigenous and the foreign," they are more clear-cut "mix and match" techniques derived from the perspectives of time and geography. With a certain Chinese style design motif in mind, the designers, using eclectic elements with widely different cultural contents and their contrast in styles, can create a modern Chinese style interior more appropriate for modern men to appreciate and use.

As a commonly used technique for modern interior design, "mix and match," with its flexible and balanced handling of the space functionality and artistry, and in response to the trend towards multiculturalism and diverse tastes, has been the focus of increasing interest and appreciation. One may even venture to suggest that with the advent of the age of information, cultural exchanges will break down the limits of regional or national boundaries even more completely, and "mix and match" will then become the trend and mainstream of future design.

On facing page The crystal chandelier, the decorative ceiling molding, and the tablecloth with lace trims exude a European elegance. The utensils bearing hallmarks of different periods on the table reflect a Chinese element. The combination of European and Chinese elements in this space is perhaps also reflected in the glass door with a lattice design, a perfect union between Western design and materials and Chinese-style decorative elements.

Art Deco Influence

Art Deco is a design movement led by Great Britain, the U.S., and France in the 1920s and 1930s. Its first major influence was on architectural design, industrial design, and interior design, and then went on to impact all aspects of visual arts. In architectural design, Art Deco is known for its use of stark outlines, clean, geometric shapes, stepped forms, and novel materials. In art design, it used geometric shapes or robust, broken lines for decoration. In materials, it boldly used new materials such as steel and glass as well as luxurious furnishings to create a more upscale feel. In color composition, it stressed vivid pure colors, contrast colors, and the metallic color spectrum to emphasize the contemporary influence. Art Deco is regarded as an art style that gives equal emphasis to elegance, functionality, and modernism.

The encounter of Art Deco and Chinese design dates back to the Shanghai of the 1930s. As the earliest and the largest cosmopolitan city in China, Shanghai had never been so open and ready to absorb the latest fashion of the world in all areas, and Art Deco was no exception. The Park Hotel, the Broadway Building, the Cathay Theater, the Paramount Hall, and others built at the time were all Art Deco buildings. Art Deco also had important influence in the choice of materials, colors, decoration, and furnishings in interior design. It

The use of stepped forms and geometric curves, the emphasis on vertical lines, and the simple decorative details in this Guotai Cinema, formerly known as Cathay Theatre, are all hallmarks of the Art Deco style, which happens to fit well with Shanghai's urban culture aspiring to the melding of old and new, and of east and west.

has left an indelible imprint of the era, so much so that Art Deco has become synonymous with the Chinese design style of the 1920s and 1930s.

Construction Materials   Art Deco is also translated as the "modernist style," not least for its use of novel materials. Metal and glass, as the newest materials of the time, were featured in Art Deco interior design. The earliest and most classical example is the chandelier in the HSBC building in Shanghai. On the one hand, these materials that represented the latest development in science and technology, and had a heavy industrial flavor reflected a contemporary trend in design. On the other hand, the use of the most luxurious materials of the time gave expression to its stress of artistic

This used to be a common sight in Shanghai. The Shanghai flavor and Art Deco style evident in the arrangement are a testimony to the deep imprint left by Art Deco in the city.

The Art Deco style is evident in this upholstered chair, with its simple form and solid look, refined but trendy ornamentation, leather and wood combination, and the brass studs.

decoration and raised the quality and taste of the interior.

Interior Colors   When it comes to colors, Art Deco used mostly pure, metallic, and strong contrasting colors. Unlike the muted and quiet elegance of classicalism, or the plain and simple style of modernism, Art Deco was mostly interested in creating furnishings that pleased the eye and offered esthetic satisfaction. This design feature is akin to the post modernist style that gives equal attention to trendiness and individualism.

Decorative Patterns   As we said before, typical Art Deco style interior design tends to use lines and patterns that feature industrialization,

mechanization, and geometric forms. The motifs most often seen are radial structure, helix, triangle, hexagon, variations of flowers and plants, or stair-stepping and zigzag lines. These typical symbols sometimes appeared as railing patterns for stairs, doors, or windows. They also appeared on suspended ceilings and on floor tile arrangements. On the other hand, as a transition from modernism to classicalism, Art Deco had responded to modernism with its industrialized, abstract, and simplified decorative patterns, while also pursuing the beauty of symmetry, balance, and grace of the classical movement in its decorative style. Also, as an eclectic and extremely inclusive art style that

A pair of upholstered chairs with a distinctive styling and a wall painting with bright, bold colors and simple lines defines an Art Deco theme for this space.

embraces many cultures and schools of thought, Art Deco is diversified in nature. For example, we can often find Chinese elements in Art Deco style buildings in Shanghai—fret work, cloud design, dragon design, copper coin design and other typical Chinese decorative symbols. Either copied directly or changed slightly, they had become common Art Deco style decorative designs and patterns in Shanghai. Yet, it is exactly because of its inclusive nature and diversity, its definition often seems vague and not clear-cut. It has often been confused with neo-classical decoration. In fact, the essential difference between the two is that Art Deco decoration has to be simple in style and fit for industrial production; while the neo-classical decoration is mostly handcrafted.

Furniture Display   When creating an Art Deco interior, Art Deco furniture, lighting fixtures, and ornaments to further embellish the space are, of course, indispensable. In fact, the movement had scored brilliantly in the areas of furniture design, industrial design, and other broader design areas. In typical Art Deco buildings of the 1930s in Shanghai, we often found marble-inlaid mahjongg tables, teak beds with sharp zigzag railings and decorated posts, dressing tables carved with V-shaped patterns, leather sofas decorated with strings of copper studs, table lamps with metal rods, and other similar style furnishings. Every one of these interior elements exhibiting a beauty typical of decorative art and industrial technology exudes a rich Art Deco flavor.

According to statistics, next to New York, Shanghai has the second highest number of Art Deco buildings in the world. Art Deco was once the dominant architectural style of old Shanghai, and in recent years as the style once again becomes the focus and a hot topic of the design world, a succession of excellent new era Art Deco buildings also rose up in Shanghai. The architectural and the interior design style of the Jin Mao Tower is a good example. It is fair to say that the Art Deco style has, largely, shaped the cityscape of Shanghai. Or maybe Art Deco, with its combination of classical and modernist beauty, its enterprising spirit, and its ability to accept diversity matches Shanghai's character as a city, and can therefore best speak for it.

An Art Deco style is evident in the furniture and decorative elements in this interior. It follows the principles of classical aesthetics and simplifies classical decorative elements to conform to the character of industrial production.

Integration of Tradition and Modernity

Traditional Chinese interior design, with its profound cultural roots and refined decorative effects, is popular across regions and different age groups. However, people's life styles and habits have seen some radical changes with time and the wholesale copying of the traditional style will inevitably run counter to the requirements for comfortable living. As a result, the practice

The staircase with its simple construction and novel material forms an interesting contrast with the classical look of the ornamental objects. It is a reminder that while people enjoy modern amenities their admiration for classical elegance is undiminished.

of achieving functionality of an interior space with modern amenities and reflecting the artistic and cultural quality with classical and elegant furnishings has become an approach commonly used in Chinese interior design today.

The key, and also the difficulty, in the integration of old and new lies in the word "integration," i.e., the need to meld design elements of different eras into a coherent whole. This integration may be expressed in theme coherence, material alignment, color coordination, or a shared decorative symbol.

Theme Coherence   There are a wide variety of interior design themes for modern or traditional styles, so it is important to decide on the theme first. Once the theme has been determined, the steering wheel of the design and the soul of the interior have been found, and other decorative means and techniques will have a clear direction and selection standards to follow. This is also true for the integrated design that we are talking about. We need to decide whether our theme should be elegant or plain, simple or sophisticated, bold or reserved. Only then can we consider and choose in a coherent manner the decorative elements

The use of typical Qing dynasty architectural and decorative elements set the tone of this décor. The row of red lanterns hung next to the window adds to the Chinese look and feel.

The typical modern furnishings in this room serve a practical purpose, but the color and detailing of the end table, the border decoration of the mirror, and the floral motif of the lamp base inject a traditional element that gives the space a Chinese flair.

of the old and the new. For instance, if we are to settle on a plain and natural design theme, for a modern space with muted and reserved color tones and furniture with clean lines, we may choose to furnish it with a set of Chinese-style chairs with rattan seats, a red lacquer food box with a handle on the end table and a couple of plum flower twigs placed at an angle in a vase. And a simple space rich with elements in tune with each other will come into view. If on the other hand, we use exquisitely carved Qing dynasty style furniture and gold-plated utensils inlaid with gems to decorate the same finished space, we obviously will have a dramatically different effect and design theme.

Matching Materials   For the same space, a repeated use of the same material for furniture and

decorative components will also convey a unified and concerted visual effect. If we choose teak as the main material, we may also consider using the same material for furnishings and decorative components, for either the "old" or the "new" part. For a spare study with a classical style teak desk, we may match it with teak doors, door frame moldings, and bookcase framings. What needs to be stressed here is that we are not saying that only one material can be used throughout. Using only a small amount of the material repeatedly in all elements can also establish its status as the main material. Take for example the same study room, the use of teak needs not be overwhelming, the whole bookcase can even use dark mirror doors and glass shelves, but the little touch of teak framing can make it integrate seamlessly with the door frame molding and the desk.

Color Coordination   The use of color coordination to create unity is a well-known design technique. Once the color tone is decided, we will have to consider if the choices of color for decorative elements are in tune with it or in contrast with it as an embellishment. By the same token, if the classical elements and the modern decoration can achieve harmony in tone, or one is the continuation of the other, and in spite of the difference of hundreds of years in time and history, the combined effect can still be harmonious and interesting. On the other hand, not only colors need to match and coordinate with each other, they also need to go with other aspects of furnishings, such as ambience and material. One can hardly imagine how an interior with bold and strongly

This contemporary sunroom adds openness to the house and strengthens the connection of interior and exterior. The classical folding chairs and latticework windows seem to indicate an enduring attachment to Chinese tradition in someone who has adopted a Western lifestyle. Interestingly, the mix-and-match of black and white paints to decorate these classical elements gives a trendy, avant-garde look and feel to the space. This melding of contradictions and contrasts affirms the combination of old and new as the theme of the design.

Curved-back or round-back chairs are representative of traditional Chinese furniture. A re-interpretation of the round-back chair using stainless steel, which is a distinctly modern material, produces an all-new visual sensation.

contrasted colors can fit in with a quiet and graceful ambience. While a serene and cultured interior that uses bamboo and rattan as the main material can surely be enhanced by a muted and reserved color tone.

Symbol Recurrence   The recurrence of a decorative symbol, pattern, or design in all decorative elements to form an implicit clue will pique the interest of the viewer, who will be

encouraged to explore and discover. Through the process, he will gradually come to grasp the intent of the design. If the symbol used is a classical Chinese pattern, the symbol itself then becomes an important aspect of the Chinese effect. We can for example choose the symbol 卐 which has a strong Chinese flavor as the engraving pattern for screens, decoration for the wood lattice on marble ceilings, fabric pattern for draperies and other

textiles, or border pattern for marble floors. Then the symbol will become the most critical decorative symbol of the interior, a unified theme for both the old and the new.

As a mix and match technique, "integration of old and new" unites modern technology with traditional art, and it should by no means create a hodgepodge interior. As such, the determination

and formation of a unified design style is the most critical. Although we have explained several ways of ensuring unity in style in the application of this technique, these methods have in practice often been used in all aspects of interior design. In other words, only through the coordination and coherence in each design aspect and of all design aspects can we create an effect of a harmonious whole.

In this space of a "modern simplicity" look, a wooden stool with fine carved detailing and a decorative folk painting add accent to it, and even casually bring out the theme of the room.

Combination of Chinese and Foreign Elements

This type of interior design is to combine the techniques, styles, and elements of the indigenous and the foreign inclusively but selectively, and use the cultural mesh to create a whole new and refreshing design effect. In order to showcase the special effect brought about by the differences in culture, designers often choose to match decorative cultures with the strongest national or

The typical Western sofas here are upholstered with Chinese brocade. A traditional Chinese table is placed where a coffee table is normally called for. In the decorative painting, a black and white photograph is faintly discernible behind the brightly colored peony blossoms. A tray with a clean and simple design holds a traditional tea set. These are perfect examples of combining Chinese and foreign design elements down to the last detail.

regional flavors, and with the most contrast. The most fashionable combination today for Chinese style interior design is the match of typical western style as represented by the European-American style with traditional Chinese furnishings.

The Chinese and western design styles in question can be of the same or different time periods. One point that is true for other "mix and match" techniques is also true for the combination under discussion here, i.e., it is necessary to distinguish between the primary and the secondary so as to allow the design theme to stand out and avoid the sense of chaos and confusion created by overlapping elements.

Chinese Traditional and European Classical
As the title suggests, here we are talking about furnishing a traditional Chinese décor with European classical furniture or other decorative

elements to create a more distinguished and elegant ambience with a touch of retro chic. Influenced by different schools of thought, there is a wealth of traditional Chinese furnishing styles with unique features that are time and region specific. European classical also covers furnishing styles with many different features. In order to create a harmonious interior design, a match of Chinese and western decorative elements with a cultural stamp of the same period may be a rational and valid approach. In the last hundreds of years, the mysterious veil of China has been gradually lifted and cultural exchanges between China and the West have also taken place in the areas of design. In the field of interior design, we can see clear traces of Eastern influence on such styles as Rococo and Baroque and conversely, traces of Western style design features can also be found in the Qing dynasty furniture known for

A revolutionary propaganda poster and one announcing a concert hang next to each other on the wall; racks full of CDs and traditional-style lowboys set each other off to advantage. Perhaps this is an epitome of contemporary culture, marked by tolerance, understanding, fusion, and cross-fertilization.

On facing page   A simple design is chosen for the staircase while the artistic calligraphic characters on the wall are traditional, rather than simplified Chinese characters. The space houses a billiard table, a Western import, while a slogan bearing the hallmark of a bygone era is painted on the wall. Is it an unintended clash or a deliberate bringing together of incongruous elements? The answer is found in the dominant red tone of the space.

If the contrast of the Art Deco armchair, floor lamp, and radio between the ancient-looking side cabinet with a simple, traditional form can be considered as a mix-and-match of Chinese and foreign styles on the macro level, then the incorporation of classical carvings in the contemporary armoire with clean, simple lines behind the armchair reflects a close, inter-penetrating influence between Chinese and foreign at the level of details.

their gold-tone paints and ornate and florid carving and its interior design. One may conclude that they share the same artistic spirit. To marry these Chinese and Western style furniture and decorative elements will certainly enrich the interior with multicultural features and interesting contrasts, and give it a unified design theme that links the Chinese cultural line with the Western one in perfect alignment.

Chinese Traditional and Western Modern

In modern interior design, Western style is becoming increasingly popular thanks to its simple and clean lines, its adaptation to industrial production, and its response to ergonomics. The claim that the Western style is the basis and the blueprint for modern interior design may be a justified one. But the traditional Chinese design style, which has an extensive and profound cultural background, is just as robust and appealing. Therefore, in order to satisfy the needs for both functionality and culture, people often choose to decorate a Western style interior with Chinese design elements, adding quality to the interior by stressing the Chinese theme. For instance, in a

The display of Wuxi clay figurines, biscuit tins from a bygone era, and book shelves crammed with Chinese children's books in a European-style décor are a silent testimony to the owner's attachment to things Chinese.

simple modern living room a pair of old fashioned armchairs made of rose wood, or an abstract oil painting hung above a long table with up-turned ends made of yellow pear wood, can immediately add a Chinese flair to the interior. On the other hand, the match of Chinese traditional and Western modern styles can also be accomplished by having traditional furniture and furnishing elements made of modern materials to convey the sense of both the old and the new. Take for example the Ming style round-back armchair made of stainless steel, the Qing-style room partition fitted with etched glass, and the colorful étagère of simple design. We can see that the manufacturing techniques may have changed, but not their cultural connotation. They are not just expressions of the combination of the indigenous and the foreign; they also represent the wish and idea of people to remember and to carry forward their traditional culture in an era of advanced science and technology.

Chinese Modern and Western Modern

As mentioned before, the entire modern interior design field in China has almost been eclipsed by Western design concepts and styles. Although designers in China have been actively working on

a modern Chinese style with a distinct time stamp and cultural content, their works so far are no match to China's brilliant past. However, ever since the 1920s and 1930s, some decorative elements with a striking time signature have become popular and have often been used in modern interior design. In the olden days, these elements were utilized to invoke nostalgia. For example, the presence of an old phonograph may bring back the songs that echoed the 1930s' nightlife of Shanghai and a collection of Art Deco furniture might also make the opulent elegance of the era come alive. In the hands of designers who appreciate them as artistic pieces, some of the decorative elements have been transformed from things that served practical purposes in the past to mere decoration. The painted thermos, a common household sight in the 1960s and 1970s are now often used as unconventional vases, and a few twigs of silvery willow in the vase can indeed make a unique contribution to the ambience. A mere display of a revolutionary poster on the table, whatever its content, would create a Chinese flavor by its bright red color and the design effect of the Chinese characters.

Aside from the above-mentioned often-seen design techniques, there are also design cases that combine multi-cultural decorative styles and elements. In these cases as well, the choice of elements from different styles can only be made with the theme in mind, only then can the elements contribute to and enhance the theme. For example, for interior design that stresses a natural ambience, we may try to match Chinese-style tree root furniture, Western-style animal specimens, straw plaiting articles from Southeast Asia, and wool crafts from New Zealand. Only through a careful selection process can we create a colorful interior design combination that truly stands out.

This chest with a distinctive traditional Chinese look in a contemporary Western décor does not seem to be a jarring intrusion. On the contrary, upon closer inspection the exquisite floral pattern and the magnificent colors on the chest appear in perfect sync with the spirit of the décor.

Chapter 5
Creating a Chinese Style

打造你的中國風

It is clear, from the foregoing discussion about the mix-and-match approach, that you don't need to go to great lengths to create an interior with a rich Chinese flavor. You can do it by adding a few simple Chinese elements. To accomplish this, you look carefully at the furniture, materials, features, and colors that could go into the furnishing of your space and then find the opening that will allow you to do the job to your greatest satisfaction and with the least difficulty.

For example, by choosing one or two pieces of classical furniture for a finished space, you can magically infuse it with a classical elegance. If you happen to want to do some minor renovation, you can easily repaint a wall with a Chinese-flavored color. If a Chinese theme has been decided on in the early design stage, you'll have the advantage of systematically considering the selection of materials and the scheduling and execution of minor renovation on the basis of the overall design plan.

A keyword is a word or a phrase used to describe the main idea and central meaning of something. Thus, furniture, materials, features, and colors are, like keywords, key pieces in interior design. As a keyword has to have a clear meaning that is expressed succinctly, so then there shouldn't be too many key pieces in a design. When creating an interior space with a certain style, you choose a select few key pieces that best fulfill its functional needs and are most compatible with the existing conditions. Quality, not quantity, is what counts when choosing key pieces for your decoration project. A jumble of too many elements will only be confusing and distracting. A focused theme is more likely to have a greater impact. Using the right key pieces in a composition will clearly bring out the theme of the work. To create an interior that can properly claim to be Chinese, you need to carefully choose the key pieces for your design.

On facing page The canopy bed made its debut in China during the Ming dynasty (1368–1644). The appearance of this style of bed with a top support on posts had much to do with the Chinese architectural forms of those days, which was characterized by high ceilings rising sometimes to a height of 6 to 7 meters. Such dimensions tended to induce a sense of loneliness, tension, and nervousness. A bed with a canopy, surrounded by railings and draperies forming a snug sanctum, afforded a sense of security and privacy to the people sleeping in it. Mosquito netting could also be hung around the bed to protect from pesky insects. The railings prevented people from falling off the bed. The advent of canopy beds changed people's daily habits—they began reserving the canopy or the alcove beds tend for sleeping at night and using the couches (ta), which will be discussed later, for taking naps or lounging.

Traditional Furniture—
Beds, Chairs, Tables and Cabinets

Choosing a few pieces of distinctly Chinese furniture as decoration is one of the easiest ways to create a Chinese interior. Traditional Chinese furniture is noted for its high degree of integration of art and functionality—the everted flanges at either end of a recessed-leg painting table (*hua an*) may appear to be decorative, but in fact serve a practical purpose of preventing objects from falling off the table. The tapered shape of a noodles cabinet (*mian tiao gui*), with the top narrower than the bottom, not only enables its doors to self-close by gravity, but makes the cabinet appear more solid and stable from a viewer's perspective.

"Sensible" furniture pieces distinguished by superb aesthetics and functionality, such as alcove bedstead, three-railing daybeds (*mi le ta*), master armchairs (*tai shi yi*), drum-shaped stools (*gu deng*), Eight Immortals tables (*ba xian zhuo*), recessed-leg table with everted flanges (*qiao tou an*), scroll tables, *Wanli* display cabinets (*wan li gui*), and chicken coop sideboards (*ji long chu*), are not only furnishings with a distinct Chinese style that enhance the Chinese theme of a space, but also objects of art that attest to the resident's artistic temperament and fine taste.

In this "mix-and-match" interior featuring multiple disparate decorative elements—for example, contemporary finishing with clean lines, a wool rug with an intricate pattern, and an Art Deco table with chairs—the centerpiece is this canopy bed , which sets the tone of the interior with its fine craftsmanship and distinctly classical elegance and unifies the décor. There are four-post, six-post, and eight-post canopy beds. This four-post canopy bed makes heavy use of openwork carving, especially in the frieze that features an exquisite *chui hua men*, or an ornamental hanging lotus gate. The designer makes allowances for the needs of modern living by converting the bed into a daybed for lounging and receiving guests. This piece of traditional furniture not only adds a cultural dimension to the décor but also finds a new use in a modern living space.

Top The alcove bedstead is one of the more elaborate traditional Chinese bedroom pieces. It is a canopy bed with the addition of a buffer space that has a narrow porch along the front that can accommodate a dressing table or a commode (chamber pot). It is a cozy "room within a room" where most of the bedroom activities are concentrated. As for the origin of the name alcove bedstead (*ba bu chuang*), one theory says it is so called because of its luxury and generous size measuring *ba bu*, a homophone for eight paces in Chinese. Another theory attributes it to the raised wooden platform on which the bed rests. The platform protrudes from under the bed, forming a ledge or a tread, which one needs to step over (a homophone for *ba bu* in Chinese) in order to get on the bed. Whichever is true, the luxury and elaborateness of the bed is indisputable. In fact, an alcove bedstead was considered a major financial asset in olden times. The value of the alcove bedstead in this photo is reflected in the heft of the materials used, the fine carvings, the exquisite details, and lavish painting and gilding characteristic of Qing-period furniture.

Right In traditional Chinese interior décors, beds are normally placed against a wall, as shown in this photo. This arrangement makes people feel psychologically more secure, and establishes a certain hierarchy in the space—customarily, males would sleep on the outer half of the bed, which is considered the primary side, and females would sleep on the inside half, which is the secondary side of the bed. This differentiation is also an indication of the men's protectiveness toward their women, and reflects Confucian ethics and etiquette by establishing order in an interior space. The alcove bedstead in this photo is as lavishly appointed as the previous one, with intricate carvings on the railings, the bedposts, the aprons and spandrels, and the panels. But this bed has cleaner lines and a more subdued color tone, and the adoption of the auspicious Buddhist swastika symbol as a primary decorative motif adds a rich cultural aura to the posh furniture.

Left Couch is a very ancient form of furniture. It has a flat rectangular top resting on four short legs. The couch in this photo, called a couch bed (*luo han chuang*), is a basic couch with three railings added to it. As mentioned before, following the invention of the canopy and alcove bedsteads, people took to lounging and napping on the couch and this kind of couch beds. In the Ming and Qing dynasties, the couch bed was also used for guest seating. It proved a comfortable setting for conversation and rest. In the hierarchy of traditional furniture, beds have a higher ranking than chairs and stools, therefore an offer to seat a guest in a couch bed was a show of respect and affection. A *kang* table is shown resting on the couch bed in the photo. Since there is step or tread, which is normally used to help people get into bed, it is a clear sign that, in this instance, the bed is used solely for seating guests and for lounging, not for sleeping.

Bottom The chair chair with its back consisting of evenly spaced spindles (*bi geng yi*) first made its appearance in the Ming dynasty. The back of the chair in this photo is slightly bent backwards at the top, reflecting a Qing dynasty influence and contemporary aesthetics. The spindles continue from the back to the spandrels under the armrests. Together with the natural wood color and grain, this design stands out in its simplicity and delicateness. The spindle chair and the window with a lattice pattern in the background, both characterized by simple, clean lines, and the entire simple elegance of the interior space, combine to create an understated ambience.

On previous page Unlike the four-protrusion official's-hat armchair, the *nan guan mao yi*, or southern official's-hat armchair, does not have protruding ears either at the ends of the crest rail or at the ends of the armrests. It has a mellow southern charm. The elaborately carved splat and apron of the southern offical's-hat armchair accentuate its airy grace. Like the chair, other decorative elements in this interior, such as the flat-top writing desk, the wooden boxes stacked one above the other, the latticed floor-length window, the cool shades outside and the white lilies in the vase indoors, and even the trees, are very much in tune with the personality of this space, which is characterized by a simple grace and a refreshing, cool classical appeal. The tranquil, cool zen-like environment quietly inspires and soothes.

Top *Guan mao yi*, or an official's-hat chair, is so named because the protruding ears of the top rail resemble the two wing-like flaps on an official's hat worn by a Song dynasty mandarin. Since the two armrests also stick out at the front ends, this kind of chair is sometimes called a four-protrusion (*si chu tou*) official's-hat chair. Its solidity and airy grace reflect an influence of the Confucian preference for the square shape and symmetry. The official's-hat armchair is not only representative of Song-period furniture, but also a classical example of traditional Chinese furniture that has remained popular to this day. The official's-hat armchair paired with the square table (display stand) in the photo creates a Chinese effect in the interior. The delicate birdcage, the brocade art on the table, and the window with floral carvings complement the decorative theme and complete the picture of the Chinese decorative style.

Bottom Armchair with curved rest (*quan yi*) is an exquisite specimen of traditional Chinese furniture. Its sensible aesthetic design and comfort and durability have won acclaim among designers, both Chinese and foreign. This design assures full support for the arms of the person sitting in it, and enables the person to relax and rest. The ergonomic S- or C-shaped splat adds to the comfort. The chair with its simple and elegant form can pass for either a traditional or a modern piece because it exudes a traditional spirit and appeals to modern aesthetic tastes. Both the chair and the ink painting in the photo exhibit simplicity in tune with modern decorative styles. But at the same time, they add cultural interest to the interior space, helping to create a unique Chinese flair.

On facing page The round stool in this photo has a sensuous form consisting of a recessed waist and cabriole legs. In the tradition of ornate and fine details of Qing dynasty furniture, the stool features red paint and floral patterns for a lavish look. The designer ingeniously matches it with a rattan screen whose spiral tendrils are an exaggerated abstraction of the round stool's curves, establishing a subtle link between the two. On the other hand, the simple, natural, and crude color and style of the screen form an interesting contrast with the finely crafted stool. The tea articles and the vase, whose styling could pass for either ancient or contemporary, are an apt reflection of the decorative theme, which stresses "combining old and new," quietly putting a seal on the design.

Left In this quintessential Chinese environment of slender bamboo stands, weeping willow trees, whitewashed walls, dark gray tiles, and southern drizzle, the porcelain table with a group of drum stools is a perfect fit. Outwardly, the material used is porcelain, which is eminently qualified to speak for China. The colors are blue and white, which are inspired by Chinese ink painting. The pattern of interlocking lotus branches is expressive of a classical style and profound meaning. The round supple forms are a feast for the eyes. The designer has taken great pains to make sure that this suite of furniture echoes and reinforces the style of the environment. Metaphorically, the fine texture of porcelain, the understated elegance of the blue and white pattern, the deep meaning implicit in the scrolling lotus design, and the tolerance and inclusiveness implied by the roundness of forms are snapshots of the Chinese identity. The attention to detail and the quiet persistent pursuit of perfection also reflect a distinctly Chinese approach to life.

Bottom Unlike chairs, stools do not have armrests or backrests. They were originally used as treads, or steps to raise one's height, hence the name *deng* in Chinese, meaning "for stepping on." Chairs have directionality, while stools don't, and therefore can be placed any which way. Their form can also be more casual. The drum stools are obviously named for their shape resembling a cylindrical drum. In earlier times, people used to place embroidered covers over drum stools and they acquired the alternative name of *xiu dun*, or embroidery-covered stools. The vestige of the embroidered covers can still be seen in the stools in the photo. The blue and white floral pattern with the punctured coin on the stool top now takes the place of the embroidered cover. The apertures and the double coins, which have retained the style of the exquisite embroidery, together with the blue and white pattern on the sides, enhance the value and quality of the furniture as a whole.

Above Experts believe that stool seats evolved from a rectangular shape to a square shape through the Ming and Qing dynasties. Over time, stools became more decorative, and drum stools, stools with oval tops, prunus-shaped, and crab apple flower-shaped seats appeared. Judging from the material used for the manufacture of the drum stools in this photo, as well as the decorative motifs, we can tell they are of a more recent vintage—the red lacquer covering the entire stool and the intricate floral patterns are hallmarks of Qing-period furniture. The openings in the side of the stool represent a decorative detail called medallion (*kai guang*) or openings to let light through. The stools in the photo are called red lacquer, four-medallion drum stools. These highly decorative stools, accompanied by the like-colored rugs and flower stands, form a striking but not jarring contrast with the black, white, and gray tones of a distinctly Chinese environment, putting the final touch to it.

On facing page The Eight Immortals table, with a square top, remains a popular piece of traditional Chinese furniture. It derives its name from the table's ability to seat eight persons, with two on each side. To add a cultural touch to the very mundane square table, people named the table after the famous Eight Immortals of Taoist lore. The Eight Immortals table, originally designed as a dining table, is usually accompanied by four chairs, as shown in the photo. Over time, the Eight Immortals table grew in status and became a very important piece of furniture. In many living rooms with a traditional design, the Eight Immortals table is placed directly opposite the entry door, on the central axis, flanked by two master armchairs. These, together with the altar table placed against the wall in the back, and the scrolls hung in the central hall, constitute the most important furniture suite in the most important room of a traditional Chinese residence.

Top Painting tables normally come with a large top to accommodate the unfolded rice paper for painting. Since olden times, schooling and the leisurely pastimes of reciting poetry and painting in China were luxuries only wealthy families could afford, so they naturally demanded better materials and craftsmanship for their painting tables. The painting table in this photo features a purple sandalwood (*zi tan*) color and fine carvings. It is a perfect match with the high flower stand in the corner. Possibly to highlight the beauty of these two pieces of furniture, the designer seems to have deliberately chosen a master armchair of simple graceful lines whose style does not match that of the table. This emphasis on quality over quantity, also evident in other furnishings in the space, creates a dynamic interior with a strong theme. The warm and festive red color tone of the space, in contrast to the color of the furniture, defines the traditional Chinese style of the interior.

Bottom The *da lian* desk of the Ming dynasty was a precursor of the modern writing desk. It normally has five drawers stacked three over two, resembling a *da lian*, a two-pouch cloth sack with openings in the middle that is usually slung over the shoulder. It is also called a saddle desk in some regions because of the shape of the desk. The "base stretcher" design at the bottom of this *da lian* desk not only serves as a sort of footrest, but increases the strength and durability of the desk. It is an indispensable piece of furniture in the traditional Chinese study. The desk, the brush and ink stone, the oil lamp, and the blue and white porcelain vase add a scholarly elegance to the interior. Nothing is more fulfilling than reading. For people desiring a respite from the hassle of the daily routine, this would be an ideal environment for their reading pleasure, for learning and recharging, and for self-cultivation.

Above In the nomenclature of traditional Chinese furniture, *an* and *zhuo*, both denoting "table," differ mainly in the legs—a table with recessed legs is an *an*, and one with corner legs is a *zhuo*. In furniture hierarchy, the *an* generally ranks higher than the *zhuo*—tables for everyday use often fall under the category of *zhuo*: *fan zhuo* (dining table), *jiu zhuo* (table for wine drinking), *pai zhuo* (table for playing cards or mah-jongg), *qi zhuo* (chess table), etc. Tables involving intellectual activity are mostly in the *an* category, such as the *shu an* (literally book table, or writing table) in this photo. Compared to the previous photo, which is also that of a study like this room, this space strikes one as more sober and thoughtful. In this study, the furniture has a solid look and the ornamentation is not overwrought. This study table has an unassuming appearance but quality shines through despite the apparent simplicity of the wood carvings on the apron and the spandrels, much as a man of substance keeps a low profile.

Bottom A *qin* table, as the name indicates, is a table for playing the *qin*, a Chinese 7-stringed musical instrument similar to a lute. Traditionally, the *qin* table has either a wooden or a stone top. The stone top is made of hollow blocks called *qin zhuan*, or *qin* bricks. Wooden tops are normally made of pine that has been thoroughly dried. To help the acoustics of the *gu qin* (Chinese 7-stringed instrument) and boost its sound volume, the table top must not be too thick. The tables made specifically for lute playing are usually lower than normal, but because of the narrow long shape of the top, they have a slender delicate grace about them. For this reason, the *qin* table is placed against a wall, serving only as an ornament, in some traditional Chinese décors. The *qin* table in this photo stands out in an unadorned environment with its elegant texture and color and graceful form. The white porcelain drum stool matches the color tone of the environment and its fine openwork carvings go perfectly with the antique look of the *qin* table. This is an ideal setting for lute playing, affording both visual and musical enjoyment.

Right To put it in the simplest terms, a flat-top narrow recessed-leg table (*ping tou an*) is a recessed-leg table with everted flanges without its everted flanges. The design of the table in the photo seems bent on exhibiting a simple square form by using the simplest material and removing all superfluous decorations, its only hint at ornamentation being the curved lines of the elongated bridle joints (*jia tou sun*). The equally simple form of the removable-panel screen and the mural hanging with a traditional costume motif reflect a style that stays close to life without sacrificing artistic taste. It is worth noting that the asymmetry of the wall hanging breaches the overall symmetry of the décor without compromising the classical style of the interior. If anything, it adds a touch of mischief and irreverence in a design that combines serious purpose with humor.

Bottom This recessed-leg table with everted flanges, with openwork inset panels framed between front and back legs and finely carved aprons going into the elongated bridle joints, has a strong aesthetic appeal, in addition to its utility. The pattern on the rug, the latticework windows, and the detailing on the lamp stand appear to be a continuation of the fine styling of the recessed-leg table with everted flanges and reflect the rich, fine details of traditional decoration in a simply finished interior.

Left The recessed-leg table with everted flanges, is a common form seen in altar (*gong an*) and writing tables (*shu an*). Unlike the altar, which has a more imposing style, the writing table has a less pronounced upturn at the end flanges, subtle lines, and a mellow form, which offer greater visual variety and the utility of preventing objects falling off the table—literati of olden times often viewed hand scrolls of painting and calligraphy placed unfolded on a recessed-leg table with everted flanges whose upturned ends kept the scroll in place, thus avoiding damage to the artwork. The designer of this interior obviously chose this recessed-leg table with everted flanges for its aesthetic quality, matching it with two like-styled food baskets with a carrying handle that have a simple form with fine decorative details. Together they create a heightened decorative effect of antique elegance. These objects reflect the attention to detail in the traditional Chinese art of living and the fine designs of Chinese furniture.

Bottom The table with the terminations was a latecomer to the family of traditional Chinese furniture. Its earliest form was the narrow *kang* table of northern China, rounded in form and low in profile. Its popularity grew in southern China because of its graceful form. Its size grew as it was used in new ways. The scroll table in this photo has a very interesting medallion in each of its short sides—a hollow-carved peach enveloping a *ruyi* head-form cloud. These carvings with a few simple flowing lines signal double good luck because people associate the peach with the celestial peaches of folklore, which are associated with longevity in the popular belief. The *ruyi* head-form clouds are supposed to ensure your wishes are fulfilled (*ru yi*) and you will be blessed with *yun* (good fortune), which is homophonous to *yun*, meaning "cloud." Therefore, the medallion stands for longevity, fulfilled wishes, and good fortune.

On facing page In the section on beds and couches, mention was already made of the *kang* table, which has a low profile and is used mainly on the *kang* (raised platform heated from below). Given where it is used, it has a reduced height and does not need to have a safety feature to prevent objects from falling off the table. Therefore, it is usually made with a flat top or in the form of a scroll-termination table, and generally features rounded lines to facilitate close contact and frequent use on the *kang*. This *kang* table is placed on a couch bed for guest seating. On the table is a cup, a tray, an opium pipe, and a snuff bottle. This leisurely picture, once a common sight in residences of wealthy families in the late Qing period, has seen its fraught history fade. Only the fine craftsmanship, nostalgic air, and residual cultural value of the furniture still evoke reminiscences and reflections about an era long gone.

Above The trestle tables supported on two separate stands (*jia ji an*) are long tables normally composed of three dismountable pieces. The design facilitates disassembly and moving. The trestle table shown in this photo features everted ends like *qiao tou an* tables but is typically less ornate than these. As a contemporary piece retaining the core form of traditional furniture and shedding the ornate decorative details, this trestle table with clean lines goes nicely with the modern style of the décor. The designer can be seen to have chosen a pine bonsai redolent of traditional culture to complement the subtle classical tone of the furniture, thus elevating the entire ambience from a plain and simple décor to one of a minimalist inspiration.

Bottom This is a traditional Chinese-style clothes rack. In Chinese antiquity, clothes were soft, two-dimensional affairs, unlike their modern counterparts, which feature hard linings and 3-dimensional tailoring. Therefore, traditional clothes racks were less for hanging clothes to retain their form than for draping them. The traditional clothes rack in the photo is an admirable piece of art craft, with flowing lines and delicate details. The cross panel carved in openwork with persimmon calyx motifs stands out with a fine carving skill and an exquisite pattern. The persimmon calyx motif is in the form of a quatrefoil or cinquefoil floret. As a result of the ancient Chinese belief that the persimmon tree had one of the strongest root systems of all trees, the persimmon became a constant in architectural patterns and plans. Additionally, the Chinese word for persimmon— *shi*—is homophonous with the word for business, therefore the persimmon calyx is considered to symbolize "brisk business."

Above The bathroom was an alien concept to the ancient Chinese, who normally placed a washbasin stand, like the one in the photo, in a corner of their bedroom for their cleaning and grooming needs. Although the washbasin stand in the photo is unpainted, the fine openwork carving conveys a classical impression—the cloud-form motif is a traditional Chinese pattern that signals good fortune and stands for a celestial world far removed from the mundane world. The application of the rain-inducing cloud-form motif as an ornament on an object associated with water is particularly apt. Moreover, the cloud-form motif has broad appeal because it implies soaring to prominence and succeeding with flying colors. With changing life habits, the washbasin stand has fallen into disuse. The designer puts it to creative use by placing a fishbowl on it. This novel and interesting idea helps elevate the cultural content of the interior with the aid of the finely made period piece.

On facing page The rack for hanging Chinese writing brushes (*gua bi jia*, or *bi gua*) is an article of traditional Chinese stationery that features a cross piece at the top with evenly spaced tiny hooks for hanging brushes. It looks like a miniature clothes rack, but the reduced size does not diminish the artistic aspiration. The rack in this photo, for example, features twin *loongs* at the ends of the top rail as well as in the openwork inset panel at the bottom. Despite their simple form, these ornamental *loongs* radiate authority. The *loong*, which is often associated with China, is a mystical beast of multiple traits; it symbolizes supreme authority, good fortune, harmony with nature, happy life, and striving. Although invariably translated as "dragon," the Chinese *loong* is really quite different from what the Western dragon stands for. The use of the *loong* motif on stationery is intended to inspire people to constantly strive for higher achievement.

Above The main function of a flower stand (*hua ji*) is a support for potted plants, flowers and bonsais. It is often used in symmetrical pairs or placed in a corner as an accent. Depending on the ornamental potted flowers, the stand can be taller or lower, square or round. It in the photo is a tall square flower stand, with a subdued color finish, delicate lines, and a simple form. The aprons carved in openwork appear to form part of the body of the stand. The artistic value of the blue and white porcelain jar with floral patterns is accentuated by the stand, which draws attention to the vase. Note the style similarities of the detailing on the stand, the intricate pattern on the porcelain jar, the wood latticework window, and the carved faceplates of the door pulls. These are unusual contrasts between the worn look of the blotched plank doors and the wrinkled couplet. It is a reminder of the ephemeral nature of human existence and the eternal appeal of art.

Above This is a piece of contemporary furniture resembling a traditional noodles cabinet. The tapered cabinet is the quintessential Ming dynasty cabinet, with the top narrower than the bottom. Its door panels, designed with the hinges leaning inward, could self-close slowly from the open position. The cabinet in this photo has discarded this obviously ingenious design and decided to retain only the external design of the tapered cabinet, which uses a visual illusion to make the leaning sides appear plumb to people approaching it. The downside to this unusual shape is that it took up much space. This led to its decline in the Qing dynasty until the line was discontinued altogether.

Right The *Wanli* display cabinet is a common name for a kind of display cabinet (*liang ge gui*). *Liang ge* is the open shelf of a cabinet. The design and manufacture of the *Wanli* display cabinet was a direct result of a surge in antique collecting in that period; the open shelf near the top was designed specifically for the display of antiques. Normally, a *Wanli* display cabinet features one or two open shelves. The cabinet here has two open shelves, which have been converted to bookshelves in this instance. The designer uses an eclectic combination of a contemporary Art Deco floor lamp, a piece of Ming-style furniture, and an even more ancient scroll painting on the wall to showcase the special charms of traditional culture peculiar to different eras, illustrating the rich culture of China's long history with multiple period pieces of the finely made period piece.

On previous page The curio cabinet (*duo bao ge*), a cabinet designed exclusively for the display of antiques, made its appearance in the reign of Emperor Qianlong of the Qing dynasty, when there was a resurgence of antique collecting. In the past the curio display cabinets were often designed and arranged in mirror symmetry. Given its long history and fine craftsmanship, the curio cabinet shown in this photo is no longer just a piece of practical furniture but has become a collectible antique in its own right. The fine carvings adorning the cabinet show not only superior technical expertise but also deep cultural connotations, which are reflected in the auspicious symbols and patterns in the carvings, such as the *shou* (longevity) character in medallion form,

the Buddhist swastika mystic knot, the dragon, the cloud and the gourd motifs, all of which represent people's pious hopes for health, wealth, success, and a happy family. The beautiful convergence of such a wealth of decorative elements on the façade of the cabinet is further proof of the high level achieved by traditional Chinese furniture in its cultural content, design, and craftsmanship.

Above This kind of compound wardrobe (*ding xiang gui*) is a massive cabinet commonly seen in traditional Chinese furniture. It is also called a four-piece cabinet (*si jian gui*) because it is a compound wardrobe in four parts, consisting of two lower cabinets and two smaller upper cabinets. It has a large storage capacity and its mass is strongly suggestive of wealth and abundance. For this reason, the compound wardrobe eventually became one of the most significant financial assets of a Chinese household. The age of the piece has obscured the subject depicted in the colored painting on the cabinet, but we can surmise that every picture represents a particular scene in the same story. The *shou* (longevity) character patterns at the bottom allow us to conclude, with confidence, that the story must have an auspicious meaning. This piece has a simple grace and the red lacquer and color drawings are typical of Qing-style furniture.

Top According to the conventional classification of traditional Chinese case furniture, a *gui* is a cabinet with vertical doors and a *xiang* is a chest with a top lid. The piece in this photo is called a *li gui*, a tall cabinet, because of its tall profile. It stands out as the star of the interior space amid the much simpler furnishings around it. The red background accentuates the cabinet's Chinese flavor. The front of the cabinet is a splendid display of relief carvings of folklore scenes (from bottom to top) of "dragons rising out of the ocean," "dragons riding auspicious clouds", and "dragons flying in the sky." In ancient Chinese legend, the dragon is a mystical beast, capable of becoming visible and invisible at will, of soaring into the sky and diving into deep water, and of seeding clouds and making rain. It is a symbol of imperial power in antiquity, and emperors of every dynasty claimed to be a dragon and had his utensils decorated with the dragon design. This tall cabinet is palpably Chinese both in form and in the motifs ornamenting it.

Bottom The color of this *xiang zi* chest complements the ambient color and its traditional Chinese style enriches the decorative elements of the interior. The use of furnishings or ornamental elements is often a quick and effective way to define a decorative style in a simply finished contemporary interior. In this interior, the designer creates a mix-and-match effect with the Spanish bullfighting poster and the clothes chest with a picture-of-a-hundred-boys motif. The two distinct styles—one Chinese and one Western—find a meeting point in the fact that both represent countries with a long history and a rich cultural tradition. The placement of a chest originally designed for storing clothing by the bed in place of the usual night table is both appropriate and practical. It shows the designer's ability to balance functionality and aesthetics.

Above This chest acquires a new role as a TV stand. From its dimensions, one can tell it is a piece of retro-style contemporary furniture. The designer has chosen the chest probably because it fits in admirably with the ambience—in this interior space all furnishings are simple and contemporary in form without sacrificing classical elegance in their details and flavor. The elaborate pattern on the rug and the framed painting on the wall, the graceful curves of the food vessel, and the sober color tone of the flower container combine to define the theme of the space, which is characterized by a simple design with a classical elegance. The ring pull and lock on the chest, made of a classical material, and featuring auspicious motifs, flowing lines, and fine crafting, paint an emphatic but harmonious stroke in the décor.

Above In this interior, the pair of bookcases is less the thematic element of the space than a member of the space that is indispensable for the creation of the design style—everything is emphatically traditional Chinese in style, from the matching furniture to the decorative objects on the table to the calligraphy work on the wall to the way the books are arranged on the shelves. The yellow rosewood (*huang hua li*) color of the bookcases blends into the ambient color scheme, their delicate forms and graceful decorations conform to the function of the study and the style of its décor. The use of twin bookcases and their symmetrical placement reflect Confucian aesthetics. This décor is traditional Chinese par excellence.

Right The *jia ge* shelf unit was a relatively recent addition to traditional Chinese furniture. Compared with book chests and book cabinets with lids or doors, it has the advantage of easy access, but dust collection and visible clutter are a problem, which is often remedied by the addition of gauze screens. In this photo, the shelf unit stands out in the décor, not only because of the strong contrast between its dark wood tone and the main color theme of the space, but also because of the contrast between its typical traditional style, fine craftsmanship, and the simple contemporary finishing of the room. In such circumstances, you need something to bridge the difference. Here, the designer chose a few stems of *fugui* (wealth and power) bamboo as the bridge. Bamboo, with its cultural connotations, connects with the bookcase, which has a traditional style. On the other hand, the container and the random way in which the bamboo stems are arranged in the container are clearly contemporary. With this decorative element that bridges the different styles, clash is harnessed to become the theme and differences become highlights. The resulting design is a pleasant surprise.

On facing page This cabinet is a kind of chicken coop cabinet popular in south China. The openwork lattice doors recall a chicken coop, hence the name. In the warm and humid south, this kind of furniture with good ventilation is either used for food storage or as book cabinets. The cabinet in the photo, placed in a dining space, is obviously used in the former capacity. In this décor with a "combining-old-and-new" theme, the lattice doors of the cabinet coexist harmoniously with the simpler lines in the rest of the cabinet, and its classical, ancient form complements the style of the lamphanger side chair. All the wood elements of the interior are of one color tone, which matches nicely the light beige of the drapery, providing the basic tone and background for a harmonious mix-and-match design.

Above *Lian er* means two drawers side by side. The piece of furniture shown here can therefore be rightfully called a *lian er chu*, a two-drawer coffer. Its aprons and spandrels are much less elaborate than those in the previous photo, both in decoration and the material used. It looks more like an heirloom, its nostalgic value far outweighing its value as art or a collector's item. Using a muted color tone for the interior, a simple bed, and a food container in everyday use, the designer succeeds in creating a cozy atmosphere.

On facing page This two-drawer coffer is a piece of compound furniture, combining features of a table and a cabinet or a chest. It has remained popular to this day because it is visually pleasing and practical. In this coffer in the form of a recessed-leg table, the drawers have been downsized to make room for the spandrels carved with cloud-form patterns, which highlight the beauty of the recessed-leg table. The finely carved face plates and knobs on the panel doors and drawers are copper fittings that accentuate the artistic value and traditional flavor of the furniture. In addition to the distinctly Chinese furniture that brings out the Chinese theme of the space, the symmetrical placement of the lamps and the classical Chinese decorative art objects also contribute to the Chinese flair and classical elegance of the interior.

Above This cabinet borrows the form of a traditional table with everted ends and assumes the dual role of a stand and a cabinet, to better meet the needs of modern living. The aprons and spandrels, originally designed for weight bearing only, have been carved in openwork to become an exquisite decorative motif. This is a common feature in finer traditional Chinese furniture—the grapes symbolize fertility and the flowing, twining tendrils and vines symbolize longevity and prosperity. The antique-looking cabinet coupled with the red couplets on the wall imbues the interior with a rich Chinese flavor.

Building Materials with Distinct Personalities—
Wood, Bamboo and Stone

The traditional Chinese style chooses and uses materials in certain characteristic ways. It is very good at local sourcing of materials used for interior decoration, furniture, and architectural elements. This approach is based on availability and practicality, and it conforms to the ancient Chinese concept of the unity of man and nature. Stone, wood, and bamboo are staples in the arsenal of materials. Working wonders with these commonplace materials, the craftsmen of Chinese antiquity have created a rich legacy of traditional

Chinese decorative art. The popularity of these materials in Chinese design can be attributed not only to their durability, availability, and affordability, but also to their close association with nature and their personification of the qualities of loyalty, honor, and grace. Therefore, these typical Chinese building materials also reflect the typical Chinese Weltanschauung, values, and their view of art. The use of these materials for interior decoration better enables the designer to put their knowledge of and passion for Chinese culture to work.

On facing page Perhaps because its natural texture and warm colors invariably bring a cozy, congenial quality to any interior space decorated with it, or because it strikes a chord with the traditionally kind and gentle temperament of the Chinese people, wood has long been the most frequently used and most accepted material in traditional Chinese architecture and decoration. Through its frequent use in traditional Chinese decoration, wood itself has come to be seen as a representative element of Chinese classical tradition. In this interior, for example, the latticework suspended wood ceiling is obviously an important feature intended to highlight a Chinese theme. Decorated with this abstraction and variation on the traditional Chinese wood roof structure, the simple *xie yi* style flowers-and-plants patterns on the wall and a few accents of China red, this modernist space begins to be infused with an Oriental fragrance.

On previous page This décor gives full play to the attributes of wood. Through its use in large areas throughout the room, wood, with its sober elegance, encapsulates the character and temperament of the entire space. It shows that in addition to their contribution to functionality and aesthetics, building materials are also capable of conveying sentiments, abstract ideas, morality, and culture. Compared with other building materials, wood is distinguished by its soft, natural, unsophisticated, congenial, and friendly qualities, and has a sense of life and a natural closeness to humans. It's no exaggeration to say that once you understand the traditional Chinese style of wood decoration, you will understand the character of the Chinese nation and gain a tactile feel of the spirit of this ancient nation.

Above This photo illustrates the use of wood in all aspects of architecture, including structural members, interior decoration, and furniture, in this traditional Chinese space. The design takes full advantage of wood's durability, aesthetics, and workability. The unique texture of wood sets the tone for the personality of the space. Through careful selection of the right timber, painting, gilding, and carving, traditional wood finishing successfully brings out the fine and elegant qualities of wood in this décor. Because of its natural feel and warmth, wood fulfills the need for a comfortable living space, besides offering visual appeal.

On facing page Wood carving ornaments, notably the Ming and Qing-style flower panel (*hua ban*) and window flower, a papercut pattern (*chuang hua*), are widely used in traditional Chinese architecture. They are a concentrated expression of traditional Chinese culture in the field of architecture. As in modern design, these wood decorations seek sophistication in simplicity and variation in uniformity. In the door panels shown here, the wood color and grain, the simple, abstract, yet traditional decorative motifs, and the pulls forming a *shou* (longevity) character medallion make a succinct cultural statement. Using wood decorations like these as accents in a simple and uncluttered contemporary interior will add a sober tranquility to the bright, lively ambience and depth to the simplicity.

Above The designer of this décor shows a good grasp of the personality of wood and the traditional Chinese style. Through the careful selection of the right timber, the designer aims to create a scholarly ambience solely with the sober color and graceful graining of natural wood, without adding any decorative flourishes. To communicate a sense of traditional culture, the designer did not take the short cut of using typical decorations, but rather transformed classical decorative elements into simple symbols, which are built into the furniture, in this case making two round openings as drawer pulls and choosing a wooden member with a lattice design as weight-bearing support for the glass top of the coffee table. In this way the designer has created a classical flair by using a modern technique.

Top The traditional Chinese style is to modern architecture and interior design in China as national character is to fashionable "new humanity." Despite the aspirations to an unbridled and unconventional style, timeless tradition will somehow peek from underneath. Thus, in modern architecture and interior design, the warmth of wood is often employed to soften the hard edge of overly stark décors. This detail reflects the Chinese aesthetic preference for things drawn from nature. In this interior, the lattice wood trims on the ceiling add warmth to the space. The traditional Chinese architectural structure in abstraction, represented by the lattice, is of one piece with the red wall and the *aoyu* (legendary turtle) wood carving that brings out the Chinese theme of the space.

Bottom This photo shows a totally different decorative effect when wood is used in a different way as the decorative material. The flooring is of wood, as is the furniture and even the trims are made of wood. Wood, with its warm color and natural grain, used in large areas, creates a tranquil and peaceful environment, which is just what is needed in a bedroom. An attachment to quality and traditional culture is discernible in the finely carved local detail amid the global simplicity. Simplicity and elegance, two distinct decorative styles, and the natural feel and understatement of wood form a coherent, multi-element, and multi-dimensional décor.

On facing page Traditionally, Chinese used wood to construct their buildings, and the main methods used were the *tai liang*, or raised-beam construction and the *chuan dou*, or column-and-tie beam construction. The space shown in this photo is probably based on the *chuan dou* construction, improved upon by the use of modern construction technology, and combined with the *tai liang* method to expand the interior space. All the wood beams are carved with beautiful phoenix and auspicious cloud-form patterns. Even without the aid of traditional furniture, the well-preserved timber frame and structural members are enough to give the space a strong hint of traditional culture.

Above The combined use of wood and stone is common in traditional Chinese decoration. On the one hand, there is a sharp contrast between the supple, fine-textured, warm wood and the hard, rough, and expensive stone. On the other hand, both are drawn from nature, which sits well with Chinese aesthetics and values. In their combined use the designer achieves harmony out of contrast and unity in diversity. The hardstone inlays in the back railing of the couch bed, shown here, break the monotony of the all-wood construction with their brighter color, and elevate the artistic taste and cultural flavor of the furniture with marbling that suggests a Chinese landscape ink painting.

On facing page The décor in this photo encapsulates the multiple uses of wood, a material closely associated with the Chinese style, in the creation of a traditional Chinese environment. Its use in carpentry, joinery, decoration, and furnishings transfers the classical elegance of wood to the entire space. The openwork carvings, bas-relief, and line carvings put the refinement of the décor on full display. The varnished wood veneers set off the carvings and add a touch of sober elegance to the ambience. The combined use of wood and stone in the hanging panel and the square table increases the diversity of decorative elements and elevates the artistic and cultural taste of the décor.

On facing page With its characteristic nodes and slender straightness, bamboo can create a unique textured look when segments of it are arranged together. In this photo, textured sections of different lengths and orientations are fitted together to form an interesting and visually striking parquet pattern on the wall. Bamboo exudes a natural unadorned charm as decoration and the densely arranged bamboo strips conjure images of a lush bamboo grove in the balmy tropics. The bamboo-veneered doors of the lavatory vanity and the wooden top accentuate the tropical mood and natural feel of the décor. Ornaments like the porcelain basin with a floral pattern and the fine carved decorative element in the form of a hanging lotus gate give this natural feel a Chinese character.

Above In traditional Chinese culture, the evergreen bamboo symbolizes perseverance and integrity, which are qualities of an ideal Confucian man. The free-spirited grace of the bamboo plant is suggestive of the spirit of the literati. The common folks associate *zhu zi* (bamboo) with the homophonous *pao zhu*, or firecrackers for festive occasions, from which is derived bamboo's connotation of good luck. Bamboo is clearly popular with all walks of life in China. The auspicious symbolism and the special qualities of bamboo make it a widely used element in traditional interior decoration. This bamboo partition adds a natural texture and warmth to the contemporary décor. Showing a post-modern influence, the partition is painted a vermilion color, which stands in sharp contrast with the green normally associated with bamboo. As a typically Chinese color, vermilion becomes a visual focus in an achromatic ambience and adds a cultural accent.

Bottom Bamboo is only one of the decorative elements used in this door, but it plays a very important part in creating the overall effect. Bamboo is used for more than half of the area of the door, forming with the wooden part an asymmetrical pattern. The texture of the bamboo has a stronger visual impact than the smoothness of the wood. Against the natural color of the wood, the bamboo painted in white stands out. The designer has put a lot of thought into the contrast and mix-and-match of different elements—the rectangular shape of the door in contrast to the roundness of the face plate of the lock; the unadorned materials in contrast to the fine decorative details; a contemporary design versus a classical décor, etc. Even the gap above the door represents a contrast of "invisible versus visible elements" relative to the door. If you take the time to savor it, you'll be fascinated by the ingenuous design of this simple door.

Above Shown here is an artistic way of partitioning space—stems of bamboo are stringed together to form a curtain suggestive of a bamboo grove in the wild. Seemingly random gaps are left in the bamboo partition to encourage a vision of towering bamboo stems in an interior of limited height—a technique used to good effect here. The bamboo, whose green color is associated with vibrant life, has been painted a warm color to match the color scheme of the space, the burnt yellow being quite in character

with the low-key and restrained scholarly atmosphere of the
space. In all this, there is a quest more for *shen si*, or spiritual
likeness than for *xing si*, or physical resemblance. The designer
employs more a *xie yi*, or idea-expressing, minimalist approach
than a *xie shi*, or realist design technique. The design is evocative
of a Chinese painting and reflects the designer's excellent
knowledge of traditional Chinese culture.

On facing page This bamboo curtain is romantic—almost feminine. Half rolled up or fully let down, the soft, sheer curtain woven of thin slats of bamboo is full of grace. Light filters through the fine comb of the bamboo strips in silky rays that recall the thoughts of a maiden. The scenery outside, seen through a mist of a curtain, is reminiscent of a hesitant, bashful young girl. The elegance, refinement, and understatement of the bamboo curtain make it Chinese. The "mischievous" designer deliberately places a rough textured stone tiger with a rugged form and an exaggerated expression in the foreground of the graceful curtain to create a strong and interesting contrast that reveals different aspects of the traditional Chinese style and the richness of its artistic expression.

Right In this photo, bamboo curtains normally hung over windows are used to adorn the ceiling in a novel application of a traditional Chinese decorative element. The texture of the bamboo curtains adds a grained look to the plain ceiling and a special lighting effect is created as conventional illumination filters through the densely spaced fine slats of the curtains, making the top part of the space a bright spot in the entire décor. The bamboo curtains, a typical Chinese element, are of a piece with the bamboo lanterns, the hundred treasures display cabinet (*bai bao ge*) and the tatami mats. Together they define the decorative theme. As a decorative device, the use of the bamboo curtains embodies the refinement, exquisite detail, and an elegant decorative effect common to this décor and the traditional Chinese decorative style.

Left Bamboo is widely used in traditional Chinese architecture because of its sturdiness, durability, workability, and because of its abundance and availability across China. Traditional architecture and interior design has been able to take full advantage of the special attributes of bamboo—in constructing buildings and making structural members and decorative objects. Bamboo can create a natural, casual look in architecture and interior design. In this photo, bamboo is used in the creation of a veranda-like semi-outdoor space, which acts as a bridge between interior and exterior. The combined use of bamboo for the ceiling and wood for the beams and pillars creates an artistic effect and a richly layered Chinese flavor as a result of the contrast between the different textures of the two materials.

Above If you look carefully in this space, you'll find several decorative features associated with bamboo: the green bamboo plant in a pot, the few stems of bamboo forming a mini-landscape suggestive of a bamboo grove, the half-furled bamboo curtains, and the interestingly latticed bamboo partition. With these bamboo accents, this starkly furnished space with scant furniture is no longer plain but has acquired an elegant aura and a pure and serene Zen-like flair. Whether it is needed as a material, or used for its functionality, or for a decorative effect, or for the creation of an ambience, bamboo is no longer a decorative accessory but has become an indispensable decorative element closely integrated into all aspects of the interior space.

Bottom The first thing to strike the eye in this décor is the three lighted boxes, which constitute the principal decoration of the space. From the décor one can easily see that the horizontal decorative lines on the boxes are a generalization and abstraction of the typical elements of bamboo and bamboo curtains. The physical bamboo culms placed between the boxes give further substance to the decorative theme. These alternating horizontal and vertical lines create variation in the space; the compact placement of the decorative elements next to each other produces an interesting mini-theme. The bamboo couplets hung on the lighted boxes not only represent a continuation of the design centered on the bamboo element, but also produce a contrast in design technique between the explicit cultural expression of traditional literature and the implicit cultural expression of bamboo, and a symmetry and unity in spiritual content.

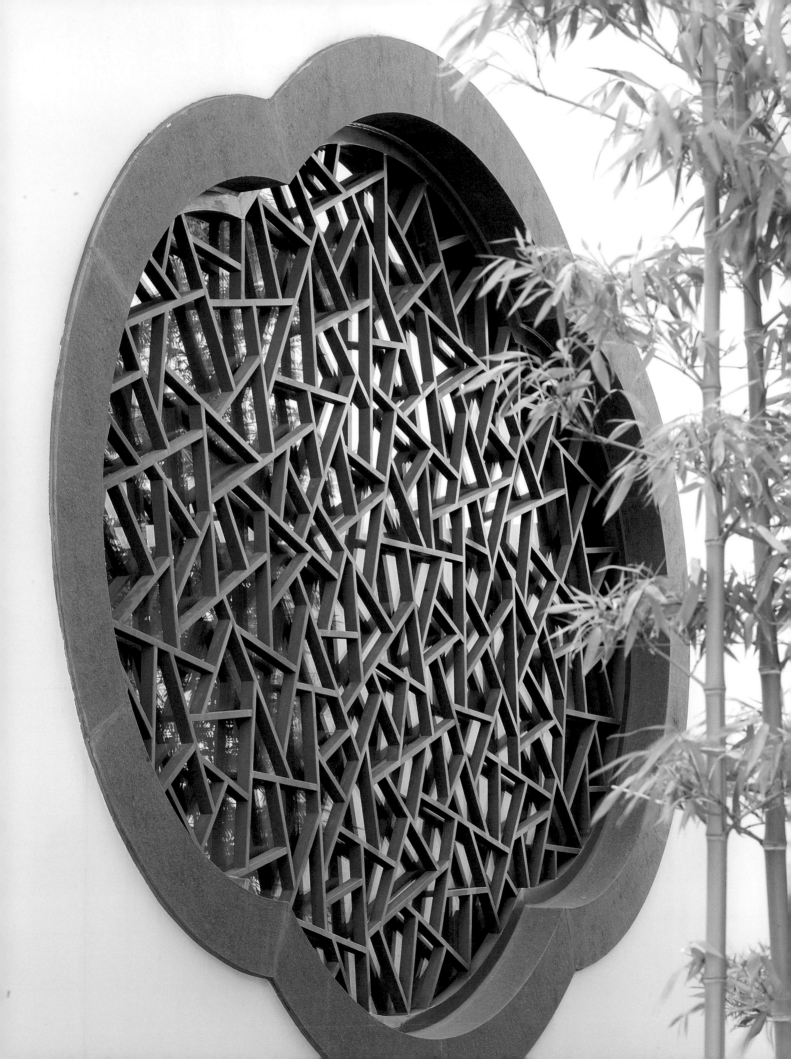

On facing page This lattice window is a common sight in traditional Chinese gardens. It features a traditional auspicious pattern called *bing shui wen*, or ice-rays design. This design, also known as *zhu wen, or* bamboo pattern, can be seen as an abstraction of the overlapping, intertwined bamboo leaves of a lush growth of bamboo and therefore shares the cultural quality and auspicious symbolism of bamboo. The begonia flower shape of the lattice window is suggestive of the color contrast between begonia red and bamboo green as well as between begonia's femininity and bamboo's gentlemanly bearing. Traditionally the Chinese like to leave room for imagination. The designer's use of this subtle way to express his ideas is in itself very Chinese. There is deliberation in the juxtaposition of a physical green bamboo plant and an abstraction of bamboo in the lattice pattern.

Above With increasing knowledge of the properties, color characteristics, texture, and graining of bamboo, its use in traditional furniture has become widespread, notably in the warm and humid south, where good ventilation in furniture is critical. The see-through cabinet shown here with grille-like casing eminently meets this requirement. The crisscrossing bamboo strips forming beautiful traditional patterns match the openwork carvings on the folding screen and the elaborately ornamented master armchair, all exhibiting fine craftsmanship. The contrast between the natural aura of bamboo of the furniture and the elaborate carvings on the decorative elements does not prevent the two from complementing each other, but instead play to their respective strength in a coherent décor.

Left This space turned recreational room in a stone grotto is visually striking. The artificial lighting accentuates the rough texture of the rock walls and creates an earthy antique feel. The combination of original-flavored painted mural and the bas-relief stone carvings with modern motifs shows the designer's flexibility and versatility. The use of a wooden table and wooden chairs in a stone environment is meant to create a contrast between a fine, smooth material and a rough one, and a contrast between an ornate and an unadorned decorative style. A common theme is preserved in the fact that both are traditional Chinese materials. Their combined use ensures that Chinese decorative styles of different periods have a chance to make their mark in this décor.

Above An inscribed stone tablet serving as the top of a tea table has to be the most striking feature in this décor. This unexpected, novel way of matching up the table and the tablet not only shows the ingenuity of the design but also turns Han Chinese writing into a decorative symbol with cultural content. The stylized writing adds a visual appeal and a cultural aura to the space. The combination of the calligraphy on the stone tablet and the traditional-style Chinese painting on the teapot reflects a decorative technique consisting of using traditional art forms to highlight the decorative style of a space. The combined use of stone and wood and the contrast between stone and chinaware enliven and enrich the décor. The contrast between the simple lines of contemporary furniture and the classical look of the cushions shows a modern mix-and-match technique.

Left top This is a close-up of a stone floor. Stone is an ideal material for flooring because of its hardness and resistance to wear. Different kinds of stone and different ways of processing stone yield different colors, grains, and textures required by different designs. Their combined use enhances the decorative effect. In this instance, the design borrows ideas from inscribed stone tablets, an art form deeply marked by traditional Chinese culture. It is a novel design that gives a cultural flair to the space. The inscribed stone tablets bring variation in color and texture to the entire floor space and the pattern they form produces a directional effect.

Left bottom This photo shows the different uses of stone in traditional architecture according to its different properties—it is used for weight-bearing walls because of its solid mass and sturdiness; as flooring because of its resistance to wear; in decorative objects because of its suitability for carving and its texture and color. The embracing drum (*bao gu*) stone carving in the photo exhibits fine craftsmanship and a classical motif. The prancing lion on top is drawn from traditional Chinese lion and dragon dances performed on festive occasions. The stylized lion performing acrobatic feats with the embroidered ball is thought to bring peace and harmony amid boisterous celebrations. The lion dance is normally the opening salvo of a festive event to be followed by shows that are even more entertaining. Therefore, the lion also heralds better things to come. The prancing lion and the dancing human figures on the drum head reinforce the theme of the design.

Right top Bricks made from fired clay and natural stone share some similarities; they are, for example, both hard and resistant to wear. For this reason, brick and stone are classified under the same category of building materials. Traditional Chinese brick carving is an art consisting of carving figures or patterns on specially made clay bricks with a fine and dense texture. These carvings are mostly used to adorn structural members, entry doors, screen walls, and walls. This brick carving adorning a wall has an auspicious flower-and-bird motif. In Chinese folklore, the magpie is a harbinger of glad tidings and the peony symbolizes prosperity. The ground of the carving is paved with a swastika mystic (endless) knot pattern, which fleshes out the picture and connotes perpetuity in a reflection of the popular aspiration for a good life that never ends.

Right bottom When selecting a material for a project, it is important not only to consider the suitability of the material for the job at hand, but also to give thought to the use of different qualities of the material to create different decorative effects. Stone is good for creating a décor heavy with tradition and history because the heft of stone gives a sense of stability and continuity, and its rough texture suggests the vicissitudes of history. In the décor shown here, stone covers much of the space, and the designer chooses a reproduction of one of the "Six Steeds of Zhaoling Mausoleum" in stone bas-relief as the decorative anchor, which, together with a stone lantern commonly seen in traditional gardens, emphasizes the antique elegance of the space. The harmonious, subdued colors and the classical refinement of the furniture reinforce in no small way the theme of the décor.

Left In this space, stone is used mainly for its decorative grain—the natural marble used for flooring has beautifully figured grains that evoke racing clouds, a rushing stream or a splash-ink landscape painting and its distinct, elegant colors make for a good decorative effect. The thoughtful orientation of the grained marble slabs point our eyes toward the entry that promises to take us into another realm. The wall in which this entrance is installed is veneered with stone of a rough texture, in sharp contrast to the smooth marble of the floor. The stone wall, the moon-shaped glass doors and the space beyond constitute the foreground, middle ground and the background of the décor and provide a contrast of three textures, all of which add depth to the space and enhance the decorative effect.

Above Would hand pull or handshake be an apt caption for this photo? First, it functions as a pull. Its shape is likely to induce an urge to "shake hands" with it. The texture, the mottled, peeling paint, and the graceful form remind us of the delicate fingers of the apsaras (Flying Celestials) of Dunhuang Grottoes. Its juxtaposition with the glass door represents a handshake between modern design and ancient form.

Special-purpose Fixtures— Floor-length Partitions, Screens and Shelf Units

Compared with furniture that can be easily moved around, furnishings that more or less stay put are custom-made mini-décors. If space allows, the installation of a floor-length partition (*luo di zhao*), a screen partition or a shelf unit for exhibiting bric-a-brac will bring out the Chinese theme of the space besides serving the purpose of dividing the space. These traditional Chinese decorative elements create subdivisions in the living space that enjoy relative privacy and independence without being totally cut off from each other. This tiered, ordered arrangement of space that ensures partition without isolation is rooted in Chinese philosophy and traditional ethics. The graceful forms and fine carvings of these fixtures have a high artistic value. Adding a specialty fixture like these to the décor will effortlessly and effectively create a Chinese ambience.

On facing page The *zhao* is a decorative element used in traditional Chinese architecture to divide a living space. This restaurant uses a floor-length partition as its public face, making an upfront statement about the kind of service and the decorative style to be expected. The decorative motif on the partition shows two dragons playing with a pearl, which is an auspicious design originating in the Han dynasty. Because of its festive opulence, the design is often used in architectural painting and on treasured objects. The shiny gilding and ornate carvings on this floor-length partition define the restaurant as a purveyor of "imperial delicacies."

Above The *zhao* divides an interior space but keeps the lines of communication open between the parts, as shown in this photo. This approach of partition without separation is rooted in the Chinese traditional concept of the "golden mean." The "moon gate" in the floor-length partition, also a classical element, reinforces the decorative theme. The grace of the ice-rays, or bamboo pattern, on the partition softens the lavish China red, and the mass and heft of the stone lanterns contrasts with the airy partition, producing an overall effect of diversity in unity.

Right This latticework floor-length partition is used as a window covering. It is like a pretty picture frame for the scenery outside. Around the begonia flower-shaped opening, the latticework is covered with intertwined tendrils and lovely little gourds (*hu lu* in Chinese), a picture of bustling prosperity. Because *hu lu* (gourd) sounds like *fu lu* (happiness and wealth) and because the gourd is associated with immortals in Taoist lore, it is regarded as an amulet that brings good luck and wards off evil. The meandering stems and tendrils of the gourd plant bearing an abundance of fruit make the gourd a fertility symbol and a recurrent motif in traditional auspicious patterns. This good-luck partition and the traditional colors of blue and yellow create a classical dining environment.

On facing page The *zhao* is used to partition but not to isolate.
In this décor however, the openwork *zhao*, coupled with the
sheer curtains, while not completely blocking the view, does add privacy, or a sense of mystery, to the space. The wall, painted a
grass green, the naturalistic tea table crafted from a tree root and
the graceful ice-rays pattern of the floor-length partition give
the space in the foreground a quiet aura typical of a scholar's
study. The bright red floor-length sheers contrast sharply with the
main color theme, and are strongly suggestive of a boudoir. The
partition and the sheer curtains create two completely different
moods in the process of partitioning the space.

Top This ceiling-to-floor window covering adopts the form of the
Chinese *zhao* and gives it a modern functionality. Although it has
abandoned the elaborate carvings typical in a *zhao*, this window
covering with a weave pattern still radiates a classical elegance.
This weave pattern, repeated in the lamp shade and another
piece of furniture, becomes a common thread that runs through
the décor. The dark tone of all the wooden furniture and wood
decorations further helps to create a fine retro style in a neat,
contemporary interior.

Bottom The principal role of this screen is (1) to create a partition
in the space, and (2) to serve a decorative purpose. Through the
gaps of the folding screen we glimpse another space. Like other
traditional decorative elements, such as the *zhao* (floor-to-ceiling
partition) and shelf units, the folding screen is a reflection of the
traditional Chinese aversion to directness in interior design. The
folding screen, with its dark wood tone and fine craftsmanship,
has a high aesthetic value. As the backdrop for the bonsai on the
table, the screen sets off the ornamental objects nicely with its
antique elegance. The achromatic background constituted by
the screen and the white tabletop works together with the green
leafage and the red sheer curtain to maintain an elegant décor.

Left This decorative element is a screen, in function and in form. The designer builds classical decorative elements such as the red beam and columns, the *dougong* brackets, and the sheer curtain into the screen to complement the classical style of the décor. The aggregation of these elements bolsters the classical flavor; and the redesign and re-invention of traditional decorative elements reflects the "modernity" of the design. The old and the new, interestingly, are opposites in a symbiotic relationship. The combination of a sheer curtain and a bamboo curtain in the screen is also interesting. They create variation with their different light filtering properties and distinct textures.

Top This kind of stand-alone, one-piece screen sitting on the floor is called a *di ping*, or ground screen. Because of its dignified styling that commands attention, this kind of screen is often placed right behind the host's seat as a symbol of power and authority and the host's status. The ground screen in the photo is striking more for its aesthetics than for its dignified styling. The artistry and fine craftsmanship of the elaborate floral designs on the two openwork panels add warmth and an aesthetic appeal to this piece of "solemn" furniture. The designer intends the screen both as a space divider and as an ornament, which forms with the stone sculpture a decorative feature that accentuates the Chinese atmosphere of the space.

On facing page In a public space such as a tea house, the clientele prefers quiet privacy. From the business point of view, however, it is not practical to partition the space into cubicles completely cut off from the rest of the space. The Chinese-style screen, which partitions without severing communication, becomes a good choice for the designer of this kind of space. As shown in the photo, sandwiching each table between two folding screens can create a relatively secure and private environment in the mind of the patrons who desire rest or undisturbed conversation. These mini-spaces feel like integral parts of the whole and there is no visual sense of isolation, thanks to the see-through property of the folding screens. Besides their ability to give a Chinese feel to the interior, these elegant screens also add depth and order to the space.

Above This screen is clearly intended as adornment for the space. The folding screen features traditional elements such as Chinese painting, porcelain, and the "blue and white" style, which elevate the artistic and cultural quality of the screen. Of these, the key decorative element is the blue and white style. On the one hand it connects with traditional Chinese painting, where equal attention to the structure of painted and unpainted spaces and the synergy of visible and invisible elements are important principles, and on the other hand it connects with the very Chinese porcelain through the use of porcelain inserts. The combined use of the three elements appears unusual and yet is justified. There is no artificial feel to the mix-and-match, with the three elements working quite nicely together. The fine Chinese painting on the porcelain panels matches the antique look of the folding screen. The painting and the classical-style furniture set the tone for this space characterized by a sober elegance.

Above We can see that this glass partition is intellectually inspired by the Chinese folding screen. We can go even further and say that it shows modern design's grasp of the essence of traditional Chinese furniture and its ability to create new forms on that basis. The screen employs an all new material and a new form to interpret the Chinese screen, fully incorporating the traditional screen's ability to partition without isolating and its superb decorative quality, thus enabling the continuation of a cultural tradition with the help of modern technology. The etched lotus leaves exhibit a grace and beauty only seen when the lotus is not in blossom. They rise gracefully out of water. They dance and sway sinuously when a breeze rises and billow like tidal waves in a strong wind. Many an ode has been dedicated to lotus leaves in literature. Since *he* (the lotus) is homophonous with *he* (peace) and *he* (harmony), lotus is considered in Chinese culture as a symbol of peace and harmony. As a decorative element, lotus also brings a sense of peace and harmony to the décor.

On facing page Strictly speaking, this suite of stainless steel decorative items resembles the partition boards in traditional Chinese buildings, but their beautiful decorative effect, articulated form, and space-dividing function quite naturally bring to mind the Chinese screen. It immediately strikes the viewer with its novelty and uniqueness—on the one hand it uncharacteristically uses a modern material to re-create a piece of traditional Chinese furniture, and on the other hand it takes the bold approach of using stainless steel, whose cold, hard and cutting quality contrasts sharply with the sense of warmth and mellowness normally inspired by Chinese furniture. The sharp departure from the norm in the choice of material stands in contrast to the meticulous adherence to tradition in the decorative details of the panels. These tensions fascinate and invite attention.

Above The Chinese character 囍 (read *shuang xi,* or double happiness) originally means two felicitous events happening at the same time. According to folklore, Wang Anshi of the Song Dynasty first coined this word to express his happiness at the concurrence of his success in the court-administered civil service examination and his wedding. In this shelf unit inspired by traditional Chinese furniture, one sees its display function, an open style, the incorporation of the popular auspicious emblem of "double happiness," the use of China red and metallic gray to accentuate the three-dimensional feel and fashionable look of the shelf unit, and the use of a contemporary material and

modern composition to express a universal wish for a good life. In order to highlight the classical style of the space and to increase functionality, the designer adds a red sheer curtain behind the unit, which has the dual advantage of adding a touch of veiled, subtle beauty, and meeting the need for enhanced privacy and space partition.

On facing page The traditional shelf unit (*ge jia*) displays objects in an unenclosed space. This traditional form of furniture and decoration is not uncommon in modern interior design. The shelving on the kitchen wall in this photo is a piece of modern

furniture combining functional and decorative qualities, featuring an open style of storage and a pattern similar to brick walls perforated with floral motifs found in traditional Chinese architecture. The color of the shelving complements the white theme of the kitchen. Its pattern is compatible with that of the wall tiling. In decorative style it is of a piece with the panel doors of the kitchen cabinets, ornamented with floral carvings. With its classical form and simple style, the shelf unit bridges the classical elegance and contemporary simplicity of the mix-and-match interior.

Above The main part of this piece adopts the form of the curio cabinet, also commonly called *bo gu jia*, a display cabinet for the exhibition of antiques and art crafts. The curio cabinet made its first appearance in the Qing dynasty and its popularity quickly spread. It is considered one of the most representative forms of Qing furniture. *Duo bao ge*, literally "multiple treasure shelves," is so called not only for its multiple shelves but also for its outstanding style, which varies with the aesthetic preferences of the craftsman and the owner of the piece. The piece shown here stands out with its resemblance to a traditional Chinese building, complete with a roof, foundation, beams and columns, and a hanging lotus gate, the whole thing looking like a miniature three-bay palace. This furniture used for displaying beautiful objects is itself a superb ornament for the interior space.

Left Its classical form, color and connotation make this shelf unit imitating a wall niche a very important element in the creation of the intended mood of this space—the warmth and elegance of the wood-toned shelf unit is set off by the dark color of the stone-surfaced wall; there is a contrast between its round shape and the square and straight wall, between its roundness and the square shape of its recessed compartments, this picture of "a circle in a square and a square in a circle" seemingly hinting at some ancient philosophy. Then there is the contrast between the yang represented by the slight projection of the unit from the wall and the yin represented by the recession of its compartments. These contrasts in details and a mix-and-match approach enrich and spice up the entire décor. The classical flavor evident in this unit matches the style of the other decorative elements and the décor as a whole. Unlike furnishings transplanted directly into an

interior, this shelf unit has been redesigned and reinvented in a rethinking of traditional culture with a view to innovation.

Above The curio cabinet display units are generally paired in mirror symmetry. The moon-shaped unit in this photo is actually composed of a left and a right unit butted together. The wooden furniture in this space, notably the curio cabinet, is generally characterized by simple forms and delicate decorative details, in contrast to the mass and heft of the interior construction, and decorative features and objects like the brick carving and the bronze vessel. In form, the moon-shaped curio cabinet display unit resonates with the round table. Its lively, dynamic form is an antidote to the square and plain look of the other pieces of furniture and ornaments of a more traditional style.

On previous spread Both the traditional Chinese floor-length partition and shelf unit have the ability to partition space into parts that are not completely cut off from each other. The partition in this photo incorporates both of these decorative features. It possesses the beauty of the partition and the display capacity of the shelf unit. In form, this partition dissects and distills the traditional designs, getting rid of the elaborate decorative frills to retain the classical spirit and tradition in their essentials. The beauty of the design is also seen in the painstaking organization of details such as the roundness of the partition versus the square shape of the shelving, and the one partition versus the many compartments of the shelving. The rows of gilt-painted Buddha statues and the clusters of red lanterns complement each other, and together they accentuate the theme of the interior design.

Top When interpreting the spirit of traditional furniture using modern design techniques, it is crucial to heed the original scale and proportions of the traditional furniture in question. The shelving used as a wall in this interior may appear to be simple, composed of little square compartments repeated many times. Suppose we enlarge the compartments to four times their original size. You can imagine the result: the exquisiteness of the Chinese style will be completely lost! If we change the proportions, for example, by using a rectangular, rather than a square shape for the compartments, it will also be hard to retain the original Chinese flavor. In this design, the simple elegance of unadorned wood is a good match with the classical form of the shelf unit; and the low-key, down-to-earth styling goes well with the simple form. Because of a good grasp of these criteria, the designer successfully integrates the classical spirit with a novel design. The shelf unit bridges the unsophisticated traditional furniture and modern interior construction, bringing harmony and a coherent style to the interior.

Above Traditionally the shelves or compartments in a shelf unit are divisions in a single unit. But the design shown here seems to take a "deconstructive" approach, breaking the unit into constituent parts and reassembling them into groups to re-create a shelf unit with post-modern connotations. The designer reinterprets the open display style of the shelf unit by using

transparent glass. Following this disassembly and reassembly, an all-new, modern shelf unit retaining a traditional flavor emerges. The minimalist dragon motifs on the base and the classical cloud-form patterns etched in the glass make a subtle, yet unmistakable statement about its defining style and cultural lineage.

Chinese Colors— Harmony, Contrast and Achromatism

When it is impractical to make any adjustments in space arrangement, materials, and furniture for a decoration job, the use of distinctly Chinese colors are quickly effective and innovative ways to change the look and feel of a space. Both elegant colors and lavish colors are used in traditional Chinese spaces. Colors are mixed and matched for different effects; in the harmony approach, a coherent effect is sought, and the contrast approach is used for a heightened decorative effect. The achromatic style typical of Chinese ink painting is another major approach in color use in traditional Chinese interiors. One of these approaches will surely meet your need in the design of a space with a desired style.

Right Harmony of colors is much in evidence in this space. It is present from the materials used to the colors of the furnishings. The designer chooses wall and floor colors that match the ground color of the mural paintings to stress the coherent nature of the décor and, in so doing, expand the coverage of the murals, infusing the space with a strong artistic atmosphere. If you don't look closely, you will probably not notice the sliding door in the wall adorned by the mural paintings, which goes to show the careful thought that goes into the creation of a unified space. The wooden door frame, the border of the mounted calligraphy and the ribbons adorning the ladies' robes in the painting are all of a dark brown, still within the warm, harmonious color scheme of the décor, and serve as a local accent. The achromatic white can be mixed and matched with all color tones. Here it serves as a highlight that brightens up the overall picture.

Top This red wall is unquestionably the main background of the space. It is a bright spot that draws attention in the overall subdued color tone of the space. Its obvious Chinese flavor echoes the classical style of the environment. Another wall of the same color in the far background, the red ornament on the tapestry, the warm color of the embroidery on the cushions, the spray of crimson flowers on the tea table, and even the sweets with red wrappers in the fruit tray, are details that are designed to match the color of the theme wall and to create, with the sprinkling of red, a general sense of the color scheme. The warm and achromatic colors of other elements in the space, together with the color red, help create a harmonious decorative effect.

Above The first impression of this space is one of elegance, an impression typical of a mix-and-match of harmonious colors. The main colors used in this space are off-white and tawny brown. They can be mixed to good harmonious effect because they belong to the same color group, the difference being in the degree of lightness. Both are characterized by a subdued elegance, which is accentuated when they are mixed and matched. The lighting design also plays an important role in mood creation—the soft light seems to apply a coat of gilt to the entire space, accentuating, intensifying, and magnifying the elegant feel of the interior and the sense of a coherent whole.

Above Red is a bright, warm color and in Chinese minds red represents festivity and celebration. Red is therefore widely used by the Chinese on festive occasions as a symbol of joy, prosperity, and good luck. The Chinese also think red wards off evil and by adorning themselves and their environment with red they will be able to avoid misfortune and be rewarded with good luck. As a consequence the Chinese have become adept at using the color red, which they come to love, and red eventually gets to be associated with things Chinese—hence the name China red. In this décor, red is obviously the main color. The color runs through the large wall areas, the silk back cushions and the bolster pillow on the couch bed, and the figurines on top of the cabinet. The classical, Chinese furniture helps create a very Chinese, very leisurely, cozy, and home-like environment.

Top on facing page The color harmony in this space is achieved mainly through the mix-and-match of materials of different colors and shades. From the off-white of the window curtain and the seat mats to the straw color of the tatami mats and the chess boxes; from the brown of the chess table and tea tray to the darker brown of the floor and draperies, these quiet colors

mix harmoniously together to create an airy beauty. Note that the materials used in this décor keep their original, natural colors, reflecting a naturalistic, fresh, and down-to-earth design style. It attests to the careful thought given by the designer to the effect of material selection on the color scheme and the atmosphere of the space being designed.

Bottom on facing page While red is the color most associated with things Chinese and is a symbol of good luck and festivity, bright yellow was in Chinese antiquity a color reserved exclusively for imperial use. It symbolizes supreme imperial power and a level of wealth and luxury unattainable by commoners. These two colors therefore represent in Chinese minds the most prestigious colors and their combined use is favored by the Chinese. Besides the mix-and-match of red and bright yellow in large areas in this décor, more evidence of its use is found in the individual furnishings. For example, the gilt patterns on the red surface material of the sofa and the cushions, the gold filigree pattern on the red wallpaper, and the red seal on the yellow ground of the calligraphy work.

Top on facing page In terms of color attributes, the green of the wall is a cool color and the tan of the wood furniture a warm one. But given the association that people have of green with trees, and therefore, of wood, the combination of wood grain and the color green feels natural and harmonious. The color scheme of this interior consists of the color tones of wood and green for all structural elements and furnishings. The freshness of green and the natural look of wood give the space its personality. In the mix and match of colors, the design mainly relies on the natural green of potted plants and flowers that echoes the color of the wall to highlight its color personality. Decorative wood utensils, a vase, and a Buddhist statue of analogous colors echo the wood tone. Note that the group of three decorative wood panels on the wall not only echoes the wood tone, but also blends in with the main green theme of the décor because of the blue washes on them.

Bottom on facing page Besides using the original colors of wood, stone, and brick to achieve color harmony, the designer of this space also makes color adjustments on certain materials to create a desired effect. As part of the principal decorative feature of the space, the moon gate, which is of wooden construction, is painted a gray green, instead of retaining its wood tone (which would have perfectly matched the color of the floor) to create the visual effect of an outdoor garden. The moon gate and Taihu rocks are decorative elements commonly found in traditional Chinese gardens. The introduction of decorative elements normally for the outdoors into an interior space is a design technique intended to create the sense of a boundless space in a physically limited environment. The gray-green color, conjuring images of lush growth, accentuates the sense of the outdoors.

Top right Imagine the dullness and monotony that would result if the few green leaves were left out of the picture! The combination of harmonious colors, while affording a sense of warmth, stability, harmony, and elegance, seems at the same time to lack variation and vibrancy. The color contrast approach takes a very different tack. Thus, in the dining room shown here, the colors of the wall, of the decorative details on the furniture, of the eating utensils and dishware, the place settings, the napkins, and the wall art closely match the main red theme of the space. But the designer breaks this unity with the vase holding a few green leaves, casually and spontaneously creating a local color contrast that injects a note of vibrancy and liveliness to a décor that is on the whole characterized by color harmony.

Bottom right At first glance, there is a contrast between red and green in this corner of a room—the red paint of the furniture, the utensils, and the vase versus the grass green of the handkerchief in the handled basket and the painting hung on the wall. But the color contrast is not as striking as in the previous example. For one, the two colors are of a lower purity to start with. And then there is the disproportion between the areas occupied by the two colors. Another important reason for this less pronounced contrast is the yellow element in the wall and the painting: its warmth is in a color phase between red and green, thereby acting as a bridge or a buffer between the two, creating a color combination characterized by a rich variety and mellow harmony.

On facing page In the color contrast approach, when the areas of the contrasted colors are disproportional, the result will be a local accent in a generally harmonious setting. If the contrasted areas are roughly equal, there will be a visual shock that some contemporary designers use to create a "color clash" effect. This is the case with the interior shown here. The proportions of the true red of the furniture and some ornaments, the purple blue of the wall, and the green of the lowboy are roughly the same, and all three are intense colors that sharply contrast with each other, thus creating a striking effect. Although this kind of color clash is not often seen in traditional Chinese designs, the colors red and green have very strong Chinese connotations and the combination seems popular with the people. Therefore, a Chinese flavor can be created in a contemporary interior by using this color combination aided by a few pieces of classical, antique furniture.

Right Without the decorative painting on the wall, this corner of the room still has a Chinese look and feel. With the painting, however, the space acquires an additional dimension: first of all, the decorative technique and the style of the painting itself inject a contemporary note into the space, creating, together with the classical style of the décor, a typical mix-and-match effect reflecting an avant-garde style. Moreover, a dramatic contrast fraught with intense emotion is evident in the color combination of the painting and in the color relationship between the painting and the space. This stands in counterpoint to the understated elegance of the Chinese style and reflects the owner's artistic and aesthetic breadth. There is also harmony in this space: e.g. the local harmony between the main color theme of the space and spots of color in the painting that echo the main color tone. And if you look closely, you will see that the painting expresses a traditional essence in a stylish fashion—thus the very Chinese colors employed in the painting, classical elements such as the flowers and even the combined use of a *xie yi* (minimalist) and *xie shi* (realist) technique convey an indescribable Chinese feel that complements the overall decorative style of the interior.

Bottom on previous page A well-thought out design doesn't have to mean a grand project. Sometimes a minor change is enough to dramatically alter the atmosphere of a décor. Thus, back cushions on a sofa, normally a secondary decorative element, definitely play a leading role in the color scheme of this space. With their bright assortment of colors, they seem to create colorful ripples that reverberate through this space of muted colors. Upon closer examination, you will find that most of the colors used for the cushions blend harmoniously with the main color theme represented by the wall. This ensures a variegated, but not chaotic, color combination. These colors—rose red, grass green, sapphire blue, and bright orange—have a strong traditional flavor that matches the antique style of the couch bed, accentuating the elegant décor intended to elicit a sense of nostalgia.

Left The "color clash" approach must not be interpreted as throwing a bunch of colors randomly together. The combination of sharply contrasted colors uses the contrast to bring out the distinct personalities of the different colors and to create with them a new, visually compelling experience and an aesthetic effect. As bold as the use of colors is in this décor, it follows a set of aesthetic rules and criteria—thus, aside from the achromatic colors black and white, there are only three other colors, i.e. red, yellow, and blue throughout. The three colors are not equal proportion-wise, and as explained before, yellow plays a buffering role between cool and warm colors. Clearly the choice of these three colors is deliberate. The Chinese element in the furnishings offers a new insight into color design in interior decoration. Here, amid a smorgasbord of colors, you can discern the vermilion of palace walls, the bright yellow of glazed ceramic tiles, and the indigo of peacock feathers.

Bottom on facing page The color contrast in this interior is different from what we've seen so far: it is not a contrast in tone or phase between the colors, but one between chromatic and achromatic colors. Achromatic colors include black, white, and all shades of gray that result from their combination. Chromatic colors are all those on the visible spectrum, with red, orange, yellow, green, cyan, blue, and violet being some of the basic colors. In this interior, the striking red masses contrast with the black and white theme of the space and add a warm focus, a festive mood, and a rich Chinese flavor to the simple, elegant décor.

Above As explained before, wood and the color green are considered harmonious colors because of the association of wood with the green foliage of trees. In this décor, however, furniture is painted a red color and the green is of a high purity, thus accentuating the contrast between the two. Red and green in a way represent two extremes in the Chinese temperament—red is suggestive of passion, joy, and good luck, typical of a boisterous dragon or lion dance; green is associated with disinterest in worldly gains, serenity, and seclusion, a bubbling spring in an uninhabited mountain or a quiet wood area. In this instance, red is found on material things, such as the bamboo basket, the cabinet, and the couch, while green is present in things for spiritual enjoyment, such as the spray of flowers, the cushions, and the tea things. The two colors, representing respectively the *ru shi* (philosophy advocating engagement with the world) and the *chu shi* (renouncing or transcending the mundane world) schools of though, find harmony in the Chinese people. This may, in a sense, be a reflection of the combined impact of the various kinds of ancient philosophy on traditional culture.

Left Opulence, gilt, and elaborate carvings generally characterized Qing-period decoration and architecture. The use of brilliant colors peaked in the Qing Dynasty. In this photo, the wood members, such as the railings and balusters of the staircase and the winding corridor, are painted a red color, which is the main color of the décor and creates a festive mood for the space. The mica chandeliers and the rugs with elaborate, colorful patterns add to the luxury typical of Qing-style decoration. The dominance of the warm colors red and yellow creates a coherent color theme for the space. The small area of emerald green forms a local contrast that adds an accent to the overall color scheme and enhances the visual appeal of the space.

Bottom In this space, color contrast is not only evident in the contrast between emerald blue and bright yellow, but also manifest in the contrast between elaborate multi-color patterns and solid colors. The contrast between emerald blue and bright yellow, two typically Chinese colors, and between their color phases, creates a good decorative effect and sets off the classical ambience. There is harmony in the brightness and purity shared by the two colors. A contrast between the traditional Chinese style and a modern design technique is present—as a contrast between masses of pure colors is rarely found in the traditional Chinese style. Color contrast is mostly found in elaborate patterns and motifs, such as in these cushions with a rich ethnic color. The two kinds of contrast create and enhance an Oriental ambience in this space.

Above The décor is unmistakably Chinese, with the colors echoing the theme of the space and contributing to mood creation. In addition to the mass use of red to highlight a festive mood, the design also uses the "five-color decoration" style for the decorative wall painting and the glass ceiling. According to the Five Elements theory of ancient China, the structure of the cosmos mirrors the five elements of wood, fire, earth, metal, and water, each of which has its distinct form, material properties, sound, and color. They represent the colors green, red, yellow, white, and blue, respectively. Contrast, mutual repulsion, and reinforcement are observed among these colors. In a sense, Chinese color aesthetics is based on the belief that colors are closely bound up with people's fortunes (or misfortunes) and their physical and psychological health, rather than on visual appeal. This kind of color use and combination is itself very Chinese and very traditional.

Top on facing page Decorated with the same two colors black and white, some interiors have a simple and spontaneous

look and fee, some exhibit a contemporary minimalist style, and yet others are marked by a stylish, cool appeal. This black and white space exudes an understated elegance, an aura of carefree serenity. Overall, the bright, white tone of the space sets off the sober-colored furniture with elegant forms, the color combination setting a quiet tone for the interior. The intent of the elegant design is reflected in the furniture, e.g., in a recessed waist, an osier seat, or an S-shaped splat. The flax tablecloth and the seemingly random spray of wild flowers in the vase add color accents and highlight the quiet Oriental aura of the space.

Bottom on facing page The decoration of the space shown is a good illustration of the statements "what seems national is universal," and "simplicity is classic." There are only two colors in this interior—black and white. Their use to describe all things in the universe is reminiscent of traditional Chinese ink painting, and black and white are never out of style across the world. Therefore it can be said that the combined use of black and white in decoration reflects traditional Chinese culture and a universal

practice. Moreover, this frugal use of colors embodies Taoist-inspired artistic concepts such as "*ji bai dang hei*" (giving the same attention to the composition of the blank spaces as to the structure of written or painted spaces) and *xu shi xiang sheng* (the synergy of visible and invisible elements) and creates timeless classics in the most succinct fashion. The line art peony blossom on the wall further crystallizes the Chinese flavor of the space, adding a distinctly Oriental fragrance and beauty to the black and white space.

Above The design of this living space emphasizes the neatness and order characterizing the residence of a "good" family in the old days. The colors seem to reflect the immaculate history of the family—the dark color of the furniture symbolizes solidity and trustworthiness and the white color bespeaks a purity of thought and soul. The furnishings exhibit an elegance of style rarely found other than in a family with a scholarly tradition. The owner's fine taste and aesthetic preferences can be seen, for example, in the cabriole legs with simple, shapely curves, the copper face plates on the cabinet doors, the elegant lamp stand, and the allegorical paintings on the wall. The ensemble of colors and furnishings paints an apt portrait of the honest, scholarly resident's classical family tradition and gives us a basis for speculating about the resident's character.

Right Although black and white are both achromatic colors, white is the absence of color and is more for being less. Black, on the other hand, is the result of the mixing of all colors; it commands the rest of the colors and is at the same time the base of all colors.

These two achromatic colors are often used to express extreme emotions. In this living space, colors are used to create a Chinese atmosphere with poetic frugality and precision—witness the black stairs conjuring images of a creaky wooden staircase, the curved balustrade to which much poetry could have been dedicated, and the antique-looking floor lamp that could have shone upon paths meandering through a fragrant garden. The black and white spots sprinkled around the room are like snippets of whitewashed walls topped by dark tiles…A vivid sketch of China emerges—using only the colors black and white.

On facing page This is a partial view of the new wing of the Suzhou Museum, a signature work by the world-famous architect of Chinese descent Mr. I. M. Pei. A descendant of a prominent family of Suzhou, Mr. Pei naturally has a deep attachment to his home town. In this building he chose the colors of whitewashed walls and dark gray tiles popular in traditional Suzhou houses to be the theme colors and to create a classical southern ambience. The gray pavement reminiscent of a cobbled alley; the hexagonal "leak windows" in a wall ushering in the outside scenery; the mini-blinds covering the ceiling conjuring images of sheer bamboo curtains. The whole space could be a painting titled "Home Town" that speaks of Mr. Pei's attachment to his roots.

Right The white in this space is like a white sheet of paper, and the black is like an inked line; together they form a picture of simple charm. The large swath of black wooden floor is the geometric "plane" that is the anchor of the space; the suspended ceiling, the inscribed horizontal tablet, and the recessed-leg table with everted flanges, all black in color, are the "lines" in the space that define the outlines or contours; the vase, the calligraphy work, and the stationery on the table are the "points" that represent the finishing touch. These black points, lines and planes, together with the simple finishing materials, give the interior an unadorned, scholarly aura.

Bottom Even in an achromatic space, the proportion between black and white has a great impact on the mood of the space. Unlike the décor in the previous photo, this space has a white theme, with black as an accent only. In this case, black does not rival with white but rather accentuates its purity. Unlike in other achromatic spaces, this white interior elicits a novel sensation with a rough, brick-like texture and arched forms often found in stone grottoes. The Chinese theme of the space is made more apparent by the sculptures of Chinese door gods and the folk paintings adorning a wall.